I0058021

Marketing & Sales – Business Value Drivers
A Novel/Guide to More Effective Marketing & Sales

By: Michael P. Gendron

© By Michael P. Gendron
Any reproduction of any part of this publication without the
written consent of Michael P. Gendron is prohibited.
ISBN-13: 978-0-9798257-6-7

PREFACE

This novel is a composite of business programs implemented by many companies – small and large. As such, it includes a fairly complete menu of Marketing and Sales opportunities that can be used to improve company value.

No one company has implemented all these actions, but I wanted to share a pool of opportunity with the reader so that you can select those that make sense for your company.

Many successful programs are the result of simply reprioritizing marketing and staff activity… hence, no incremental spending.

I hope that you enjoy the story, and try some of these activities. You will be pleasantly surprised by the results.

THE CHALLENGE

Brad aligned his 26-foot birdie putt on the 18th green. Jonathan saw that the green was table-top smooth with a double break – it looked like a warped billiard table. "OK, Jonathan, five bucks says I drop this. You in?"

Jonathan laughed, nodded his head and said, "If you took this shot 25 times, you couldn't make it. Sure – I'm in."

Brad stepped back from the putt to confirm his shot. He addressed the ball, setting his putter gently on the surface. His feet moved slightly to reach perfect balance before he stroked the putt. As the putter moved through the ball, the 'click' was solid, and the shot was true. Given the green's speed, the gentle touch allowed the ball to curve slowly through the micro-maze of break, and dropped with a solid 'thunk'. "You owe me, Jonathan."

"OK, Brad, you're a better man than me. Let's grab a 'lemonade' at the clubhouse."

They loaded their equipment into their bags and drove leisurely to the clubhouse.

"So, Brad, what's new with the business these days?"

"Same old, Jonathan. You know, I've been with the Company for …" After a moment's pause, he continued, "Can you believe that I've been here for close to 20 years. Better yet, Jackson and the other partners retired, and we worked a sweet deal so that I could buy the place 7 years ago. I've enjoyed every minute of working at this Company, when you think on the grand scale. But there definitely were some serious challenges during the years.

Those sleepless nights – well, now I wear them as a badge of honor.

But for the past year, I've become a bit restless. Not dissatisfied with the business, but thinking there must be more. I'm just not sure what 'more' is."

Brad parked the cart along the walk. "C'mon – I'd like to claim my prize with that first drink - on you, Jonathan."

Brad and Jonathan have been challenging each other at golf for about 10 years. They often would speak about business, in general. Occasionally Brad would float a question to Jonathan about growth or profitability, but they never really explored growth and profit opportunities in depth.

Brad was in his late 40's. His Purdue Mechanical Engineering degree launched his career with Precision Technologies, Inc. Jackson, the former Precision majority owner, invested a lot of time in Brad's career. Jackson, also a Purdue grad, enjoyed cultivating young graduate careers, although his employees frequently left the business for more fertile opportunities. It seems that with some of these young aggressive professionals, the business just couldn't challenge them enough.

For those that were willing to work at *Precision's* pace, Jackson rewarded them with progressively increased and broader responsibility. During Brad's career at Precision, he enjoyed projects in new product development and technical sales. Jackson also exposed Brad to marketing and manufacturing tasks.

Brad and Jonathan settled into the comfortable leather chairs in the grill room, while discussing their golf games.

Luanne, the server, approached the table with menus. "Good afternoon, gentlemen. Would you like something cold to drink?"

Jonathan responded, "Yes please, Luanne. Can we have a couple of those Mad Tree Axis Mundi stouts?" He continued, "Brad, since I'm buying, I get to choose. Have you ever had one of those Mad Tree stouts?"

Laughing, Brad said, "I've only heard about them. Quite a kick – high ABV I think. You trying to sell me something?"

"Not a chance, Jon, but I do want to hear more about this middle-age crisis you've shared. You know, that 'restless' feeling that you mentioned."

"It's nothing major – just a mild dissatisfaction with the business. Look, it's really not a big deal. We've been growing at about 5-6% a year for the past 5 years. Profits are good. Life is good overall. I've just been thinking about, 'What could I do differently?'"

Luanne returned with the dark, foam topped elixir. "Gentlemen, this is an outstanding local stout. While I've enjoyed it in several tastings at Mad Tree, it's been surprising how many favorable comments I've heard from other guests here at the club. Have you had a chance to look at the menus?"

Brad leaned forward. "Skip the menus, Luanne. Jonathan ordered the drinks; I'll order the famous club burgers… one for each of us. You OK with that, Jonathan?"

"Sounds fair to me." Luanne jotted the order, and quickly left to place it.

"OK, Brad. 'What could I do differently' is an interesting phrase. What are you thinking?"

"Well, it's pretty simple – but also very complicated. The simple part is that everything is going great. Sales and profits are doing well… the Company has very low employee turnover… key staff are earning and receiving comfortable bonuses … no major risks with the customers… There really is nothing to complain about. I just don't feel like I've left a mark. If everything continues as it has – let's say in 10-15 years, I'll sell the business for a large chunk of cash, and move on to a life of relaxation. But what have I really accomplished at Precision?"

"Well, to start with, you've survived some very turbulent times, through two great recessions – major global downturns. You've got to feel pretty good about that."

"Agreed, but many companies have done the same. And some have even thrived during those crises. Jonathan, I'm not complaining. I've been a v-e-r-y lucky guy. This Company has provided the resources for me to put two kids through college. My son's an attorney and daughter's a humanities graduate.

I've got an airplane… vacation house… happily married and enjoying the benefits of my early career. But my life doesn't seem to have any punch."

"So, what would give you the 'punch' you seek? Faster more profitable growth? Higher status in the community? Here's one for you – do you want to get into politics?"

"No thanks for the politics. I want to be able to accomplish something, not be abused by the public. Higher growth and profitability might be nice. Not that I need the money, but more of a satisfaction scorecard when I compare to my peers."

"Brad, I've got some open time next week. Shall we just get together at your office and bounce some ideas around? This is as a friend, for now. If we really get into a project, we can discuss how we proceed."

"That sounds good. Ah – perfect timing Luanne - sustenance for the team. Say, how about another Axis Mundi?"

Jonathan agreed to another brew.

They scheduled a two-hour meeting for next week, and shifted conversation to their golf games.

INITIAL BUSINESS SCAN

One-to-One: Jonathan & Brad

Jonathan arrived at Precision Technologies Inc's offices as scheduled Tuesday morning. Their Oakley offices were a short hop from Hyde Park Square. The building was a turn-of-the-century brick building, originally purposed as an automotive plant. The facility had been upgraded several times during the past century, and most recently included extensive modifications to reflect a more open design to promote collaboration among the employees.

Jonathan was Brad's friend, and he was excited to help Brad expel his funk. Jonathan's 40+ years of experience included Fortune-500 as well as several start-ups. His core experience was marketing, spending several years with Procter & Gamble, but then he moved to more entrepreneurial ventures. He experienced sales, and in the new venture companies, executive leadership roles in human resources and new product development.

Brad spotted Jonathan as he pulled into the parking lot. He rose from his desk and walked to the lobby to greet Jonathan.

" Hey, Bub, welcome. Glad that we could make this happen. C'mon into the conference room. I've just brewed some fresh Jamaica Blue Mountain Reserve Coffee. My son's a coffee snob, and he says it's *the best* coffee."

They settled into the deep cushioned chairs closest to the windows.

Brad poured two cups of coffee, and started the conversation with some small-talk. After a few minutes, he described his funk. "It's not a serious thing, Jonathan. I think our discussion might be a bit of overkill, but since you offered, I thought I'd take you up on your offer."

"So, if I remember correctly, you wanted to 'leave a mark on the world.' Nothing major, but just a lingering feeling of not accomplishing all that you could have done. Maybe a feeling of complacency?"

"That sounds true. So, let's talk… any thoughts?"

For the next hour, they discussed the Precision business. Growth rates, profitability, employee satisfaction, customer satisfaction, community involvement and many of the *soft* areas in any mid-market business.

"OK, Brad. I've got a good idea about your personal malaise. We both know that I'm a marketing & sales guy, so if you don't mind, I'll concentrate on that to begin with. Talk to me about your marketing and sales operations."

Brad outlined the current marketing and sales organizations. He talked about the leadership in each function, and some of the major activities during the past 2 years.

"You know, Jonathan, I wasn't sure what to expect today. … wasn't sure if we'd be talking about my funk… the business … the people, or what. So, when I get into the marketing and sales leadership, I might be a bit sketchy on the details. You OK with that?"

"I'm OK discussing anything you like, Brad. Give me more background on the VP's and some of the major accomplishments."

Brad discussed each VP's background and accomplishments during the past few years. Jonathan then shifted to the broader marketing and sales functions.

Brad continued. "Nathan is the VP of Marketing. He's a young guy – mid-30's - with some decent experience. He has an MBA in marketing, but until he joined us, his career was in sales management. I took a flier with him, since he has the marketing degree, and a lot of experience in rapidly developing industrial product companies. His bragging rights at Precision are his responsiveness to the Sales needs. He also does a helluva job preparing us for the trade shows. You know, getting the right collateral material together… setting up the booth at shows… coordinating the seminars at the shows.

He's a great social networker as well. You've got to see him in action at the shows."

"He sounds like a winner, Brad. …just a few questions. How much involvement does he have with new product development? "

"When the tech folks develop a new product, Nathan coordinates focus groups to better understand the market reception. He may also discuss pricing of competitive products."

"OK. When I think of marketing communications, I think of inbound and outbound communications. Any comments?"

"Not clear what you mean by the terms. Help me understand, will you?"

"Sure. I think of marketing as a key function to identify, and nurture the Company brand. By managing the inbound and outbound communications, the marketer can reinforce the brand. Inbound communications – well, that would include the focus groups. He's capturing the information from the market – although a very narrow piece. Speaking more broadly, marketing often 'listens' to unsolicited information from the market.

Social media, blogs, trade shows, national trade associations, etc. are sources of market information freely available on the web. These and many other sources of market information are within the scope of inbound communications. The salesforce is another valuable source of marketing information.

Think about it. The reps are on the frontlines of competition every day. Some companies formally summarize this information monthly.

Mind if I scratch some things out on the whiteboard?"

"Have at it, Jonathan."

Jonathan started writing on the whiteboard while continuing to talk. "Let's just quickly look at many types of inbound communications." He quickly identified about 10 elements of potential inbound communications.

INBOUND COMMUNICATIONS -SOURCES

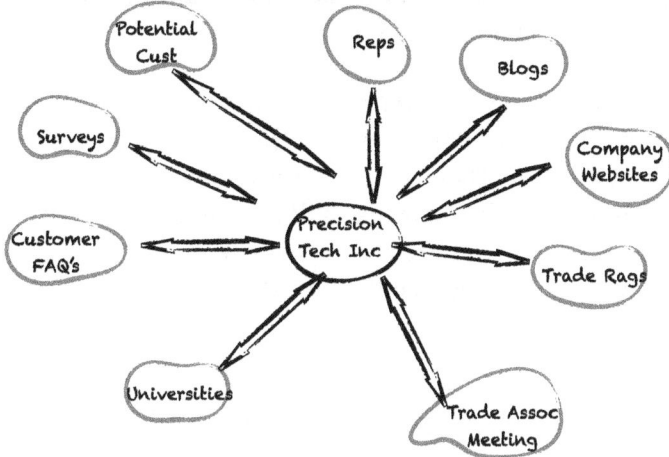

"In many companies marketing is directly responsible for managing the communication process. Marketing may have monthly or quarterly meetings with manufacturing, new product development and the sales reps to share information. As the information is shared among the functions, the team can develop opportunities to improve the business. Any thoughts?"

"Theoretically it sounds great, but it also sounds bureaucratic. Too much like big company stuff."

"I agree that it can be, but … let's hold that thought and move on to outbound communications. Outbound communications are meant to reinforce your brand, and establish a unified image to the outside world. Let me scratch out a few other thoughts."

He took a picture of the 'Inbound Communications" diagram, erased the diagram and drew a new diagram labeled 'Outbound Communications.'

He completed the diagram and concluded, "OK, we've now proven that I can't draw a circle. But ignoring that fact, what do we see. There are numerous outbound communication channels that will reinforce your brand. The communications aren't just written or spoken words. Anything that you do that the outside world can observe is marketing your brand.

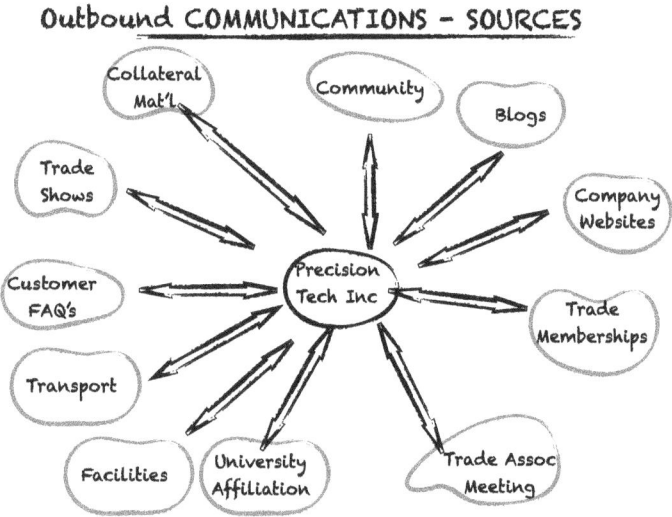

Outbound COMMUNICATIONS - SOURCES

Collateral Mat'l · Community · Blogs · Trade Shows · Company Websites · Customer FAQ's · Precision Tech Inc · Trade Memberships · Transport · Facilities · University Affiliation · Trade Assoc Meeting

Here's a quick question. What's your brand image, Brad?"

Brad smiled. "It's about time that you admitted you can't draw." Letting that comment mellow, he stood and walked to the whiteboard and looked at each circle, thinking about how these items apply to Precision Technology Inc.

"You know, I'm not sure that all these items apply to us."

Quick to respond, Jonathan replied, "Let's not challenge the individual items as much as think about the concept. Everything you say, print, do in the community can affect your brand. If your delivery trucks are dirty & rusted, what does that say about your brand? If you don't participate in the business community, what message are you sending? Brad, don't concentrate only on the individual circled items, but think about your communications to the world – your customers... potential customers ... your competitors or potential competitors... the community etc."

"You've gone too far, Jonathan. I don't like disagreeing with you, but what does community involvement have to do with the brand?"

"Where do your employees live? Where do you recruit new employees? Brad, if you run a sloppy business ... unkempt grounds ... rusted dirty trucks ... don't support the local charities ... what does that say about your Company? Every day is effectively a *job interview* for Precision Technologies Inc. Some of these initial brainstorming thoughts might be excessive and may not apply - but if you don't think outside the norm, could you be missing an opportunity?"

"I get it, Jonathan. I don't mean to be negative, but I haven't thought about these things before, and you're boxing me in."

Brad walked to the coffee pot, furrowed brow and silent.

He poured a cup of steaming coffee, and raised the pot to Jonathan as if to ask, '...another cup?'

Jonathan has been through these discussions – these interventions – before. Conscientious, hard-working company owners who were forced outside their comfort zone often rebelled. He let the silence continue, awaiting Brad's next move.

Brad quietly stirred his coffee, although he added no condiments. After a few minutes, he looked up from the swirling black liquid. "You know if we weren't friends, I'd be angry right now. But I know that you're trying to help. I'm definitely uncomfortable, but let's keep this dance going."

"So, what's your brand, Brad?"

"Do you mean what is our logo?"

"No, a more holistic concept. When people see anything related to Precision Technologies Inc., what are they thinking? Is it, "…that cheap SOB that doesn't pay a decent wage?"

"Now hold on, Jonathan. We compensate…"

Jonathan raised his hand as if directing traffic. "I know you pay well. But I'll keep going. Do they think that Precision is an ethical, honorable business that stands behind their work?"

"Now you're getting it, Jonathan."

"Does the outside world think of a progressive, high-tech and reliable vendor when they see Precision? A partner in new product development? A Company that is willing to take calculated risks? Or a Company that is so risk averse that they are difficult to work with?"

Brad smiled, "It's a bit of some, none of some and absolutely 100% of others."

"Do you have a brand statement that all your employees align to? Something that might be in your strategic plan vision?"

"No Strat plan, Jonathan."

"If no brand statement, how do you ensure alignment of all your resources?"

"It's informal. People know what our brand is."

"Then give me a few sentences that clearly describe your brand."

"I get it, Jonathan. And the next thing I'm going to hear is that if we haven't clearly defined our brand, we can't easily reinforce the brand outside these 4 walls. Touché."

"We've talked about communications and brand. Can you describe your Company strategy? The words that align the entire organization to achieve your personal and Company goals?"

"That's an open item."

"Are you a low cost, commodity business? Or perhaps a highly differentiated, high tech Company? And how do you fit in the competitive landscape?

A few minutes ago, we looked at inbound communications. Does Nathan prepare any competitive analysis? ...

summarize what's happening with your biggest competitors?"

"We don't do it formally, but we periodically discuss the competition."

"So, who are your major competitors, and what specifically are we doing to beat them in the marketplace?"

"It's informal, Jonathan."

Jonathan sensed the tension building again. "OK, let's mark competitive analysis as something to discuss later – if there is a later. Can we spend a minute on product analysis? I'd like to better understand your new product development process... and maybe how you manage the product portfolio – how you eliminate older products from the line... manage profitability etc."

Brad spoke for a few minutes about their product portfolio – aging and new product development – profitability, relationships with key customers. As he spoke, he subconsciously jotted a few notes on his pad. His enthusiasm waned as he continued.

"OK, enough about product lines. Let me share a few more thoughts. It would be great to understand how you manage your approach to the market, when considering competition. I think it would be worthwhile to understand how you approach geographic expansion, joint ventures with other companies, and how you allocate your marketing mix. That would be the investment in each activity used to promote and sell products. The mix would include the spending for direct sales, sales agents, distributors, but also how much you spend on trade shows, web sites, advertising, printed materials etc. I've heard enough to understand that there may be some upside opportunity with more emphasis on Marketing."

Jonathan moved to the whiteboard. "Here is an example of Marketing Mix."

Example Marketing Mix	Total
Direct Sales	50
Inside Sales	5
Sales Agents	5
Travel	5
Advertising	15
Printed Mat'l	5
Website	5
Trade Shows	5
Market research	5
Total	100

"The allocation of resource among all the elements used to promote and sell your products is the *mix*. For example, in today's world, a company may rely heavily on the Web ordering and reduce the direct sales cost.

Let's spend a few minutes on sales operations?"

Thankfully, Jonathan changed topic to sales.

Brad discussed the sales organization and included a brief bio of the VP Sales. He highlighted their selling process and sales operations.

When Brad finished, Jonathan focused on a few parts of Brad's discussion.

"I understand that you have routine sales meetings, and that you establish sales targets in the annual budget. That sounds like a great way to get things organized. But I'm not sure I understand how you manage your sales pipeline. Can you walk me through the process in more detail? I'll scratch it out on the board. "

Jonathan listed 5 informal steps in their selling process that ranged from cold-call to final close. As he listed the steps, Jonathan asked questions about the sale's team's activities.

"And how do you monitor these steps? For example, for the major accounts – and that includes prospects – do you have routine reporting in monthly meetings?"

"We don't like to micro-manage the sales reps. We leave the prospect monitoring and the routine account management up to the individual rep.

Pipeline & Closing Cycle

DAYS	20	10	30	30	20	110

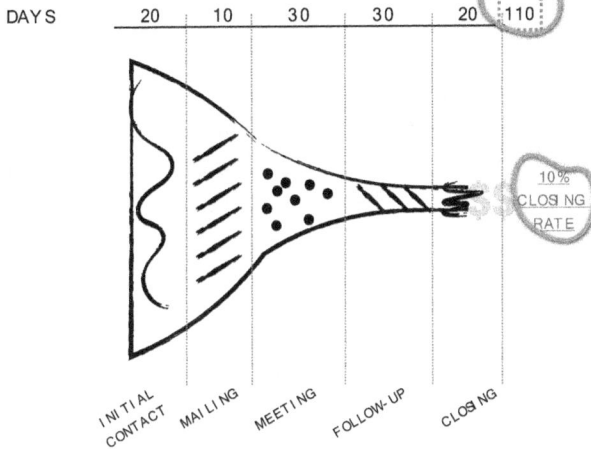

10%
CLOSING
RATE

INITIAL CONTACT • MAILING • MEETING • FOLLOW-UP • CLOSING

"For existing accounts, do you have a standard call cycle balanced against their actual and potential sales? So, for example, you may have a "B" actual account that has an "A" potential. Do you do anything different with those customers?"

"Again, Jonathan, I leave the details to the individual reps. They get a large proportion of their compensation in commission, so I let their natural drive for more compensation guide their activity."

"Got it."

"And if it's more difficult to close a new account, do we compensate that sale differently?"

"I'd have to look at the plan."

"Let me quickly draw out a scenario, and let's see where it takes us." For the next few minutes, he sketched a chart with several columns and lines.

"Let's start with the marketing mix we have on the board. I'll focus on a few items. First, we have many different ways to influence a buyer. It can be direct or indirect, and the customer can be an existing or a potential customer.

Example Marketing Mix

	A Act	A Pot	B Act	B Pot	C Act	C Pot	Total
Direct Sales	15	15	10	5	5	0	50
Inside Sales							5
Sales Agents							5
Travel							5
Advertising							15
Printed Mat'l							5
Website							5
Trade Shows							5
Market research							5
Total							100

I'll use the same metric of 100% - could be of $25 million… could be $50 million of expense. I'd like to brainstorm 'what if'… what if we changed the mix, based on the type of customer target – A-B-C … or perhaps actual or potential customer. Have you explored this kind of 'what if' analysis?"

"Not that I know of. … and maybe we should consider this kind of thinking, but it looks like a heck-of-a-lot of work."

"The organization can make it a lot of work, but literally, a few hours with a white board can capture the creative ideas that can be finalized later. Let's discuss a specific example. I've been through the analysis at a company where a rep's compensation varied from a base of $35k to $70k, and commissions that ranged from 10% to 1% of sales.

When I discussed the matrix with the VP Sales, he got too focused on the details. In the end, we discovered that the average compensation for the entire sales force was about $80k.

When he objected to using the average for all reps, the VP sales explained that hunters had entirely different compensation levels, since hunters and farmers had different roles in the company. Hunter's compensation could vary from year to year by more than $100k, since landing key accounts didn't happen every year. Prospecting takes a different kind of person. When we separated the compensation into two large buckets – compensation excluding commission; and commission – we allocated the values accordingly.

If your team were to prepare the analysis, the whole analysis could be sketched on a white board in a few hours. And then the team has to think about changes to improve performance. If changes make sense, they would then implement them. The beauty of the whiteboard is that we're not spending money during the analysis, and by limiting the analysis to few hours, the team won't get mired in minutia.

It's never a perfect exercise, but focus on the creative problem solving and avoid too much detail."

"Can the analysis be done in a few hours with the team?"

"Shouldn't be a problem.

I've used my four hours. Let's summarize.
If you really want to make a mark, let's try some new thinking. Worst case, you've invested some time, but best case, you energize the marketing and sales teams to become more productive.

Ok, I've done my duty, Brad. I've tortured you with new concepts, and now it's up to you to think about the challenge.

One thing I can assure you. If you tackle this analysis, you'll no longer be in a funk. It takes creativity and dedication to challenge your existing operating processes. Whattayathink?"

Brad sat silently, considering whether he really wanted to change. Jonathan assured him that it's an iterative process that doesn't require him to take immediate high risks. Alternatively, this analytic approach may cure his funk and improve the business.

"I'm going to think about this for a while. Jonathan, if I do decide to examine the sales and marketing, what's the process?"

"Pretty straightforward – just like we've done today. It just takes some time. We'll get the team together and talk about the business."

"Do we need to prepare a lot of information before we launch this kind of activity?"

"Are you in control of your business? Or said another way, if you know your business and the industry – products, customers and competitors – we've got everything we need to start the process. When we get into the process, we may identify things that you'd like to do. That's a decision that you get to make at the time. The initial commitment is probably 1-2 days of your VP's time."

"You've made me a bit uncomfortable, Jonathan, but I'm not sure if it's more – or less – uncomfortable than my funk. I'll get back to you within a week."

"Roger that. Hey, are you going flying this weekend?

"Flight plan is filed, and I'm off to Nashville for a couple of days."

Jonathan took the final pictures of the whiteboard to memorialize their discussion.

Brad escorted Jonathan to the lobby, and then slowly strolled to his office, considering the challenge that Jonathan presented. His funk wasn't serious, but more of a haunting cloud of discomfort. If he launched any kind of analysis he might disrupt the organization. But, given the potential for more excitement, it might be worthwhile.

Initially, only two people would be affected – Nathan in Marketing and Chuck in Sales. If we spent a day+- discussing the topics that Jonathan outlined, and the team didn't want to proceed, we've invested a day+. … not much to risk, given the possible returns.

He retrieved his mobile phone and texted Jonathan, "Why delay – let's spend a day in the next 2 weeks for an initial discussion. No promises... thanks for your insight. Tracey will contact you to schedule."

Intro Discussion: Brad/Jonathan/Nathan/Chuck

Tracey set up the conference room with two flip charts and markers, prepared the whiteboard for the discussion, and had fresh coffee and pastries available. Room temperature was set at a refreshing 68 degrees, as Jonathan requested.

Nathan and Chuck were on the way to the conference room, quietly discussing their expectations.

"Well Nathan, this sounds like the latest program of the month. Not sure what this is going to do for us. We both know that industry knowledge is the key to our success. We better humor Brad – this Jonathan guy is one of his golf buddies."

"C'mon Chuck. Don't be so negative. While I don't think that there will be anything earth shattering from this meeting, I'm always open to some suggestions that will help us be more profitable. And it's just one day – let's just call this a seminar. You never know what pearls of wisdom will surface."

They entered the conference room and poured the coffee.

Jonathan and Brad met earlier in Brad's office to plan the session. They entered the conference room – Brad with a broad smile, hoping to ease any tension that Nathan and Chuck had.

"Hey folks – what's up for today?"

Nathan responded, "Another day of productivity, Brad. I'm not sure what to expect, but I'm hoping to pick up some tips that will help us be more productive."

Chuck stoically responded, "Ditto, Brad."

Brad continued, "This is Jonathan – a guy I routinely beat at golf." He laughed briefly as he gestured to Jonathan. "Jonathan has been in the consulting business for – I'm guessing – about 10-15 years. Before that he cut his teeth at P&G, and also drove marketing and sales in 2-3 startups that were eventually acquired by some Fortune 500 companies. He's worked in consumer products, industrial products – similar to us, I believe – and national service businesses. Anything I left out Jonathan?"

"Other than I like to fly and backpack, not a thing."

As Brad settled into one of the chairs, he said, "OK, Jonathan, it's your show."

"Nathan… Chuck, it's good to meet with you this morning. … not sure what Brad has mentioned to you about today's meeting. Any thoughts?"

Chuck leaned forward on his elbows and said, "He mentioned that we were going to talk about marketing and sales. … guess that's why Nathan and I are here."

Nathan agreed.

"Well, that's correct. I want to explore the broad aspects of each function. When you come right down to it, I'm really just going to talk about what the marketing and sales functions mean to the Company … maybe explore resource allocation… You know, looking at the entire Company to see how we invest our resources.

Shall we dance?"

All agreed. As Jonathan started the discussion, Chuck stood and walked to the coffee pot – his back toward Jonathan. He poured a cup, and raised the pot as if to offer coffee to all.

Jonathan expected some pushback on the topic, and gracefully accepted this mild form of disrespect.

Brand

"I like to use the whiteboard," as he took a marker ready to sketch. "Let's focus on one word for a few minutes." In large letters he wrote BRAND.

"What does the word brand mean to us at the Company?"

Brad quickly replied, "It's who we are in the market."

"OK – good start, but let's expand on that. When people see the Company name - 'Precision Technologies' - what do they think of?"

Chuck sipped his coffee and snorted, "1st class products."

"Anything else, Chuck?"

"A great sales force."

"What does great mean.? Accommodative? Able to reduce prices on the fly? Technical sale? Help me understand great."

"Our guys are talented. Well trained sales reps."

"And is that *sales* training? Technical or engineering training? They understand our systems and how to place an order?"

Jonathan continued, "Let's say they're able to *sell* a product – highly technical because they are engineers. Do you mean SELL, or do you mean they help the customer find solutions for their needs?"

Chuck was starting to bristle at this outsider challenging his sales expertise. "Jonathan, everybody knows what sell means. You're beginning to sound like Bill Clinton discussing the definition of sex."

Jonathan was ready for the challenge. "Would you agree that there are different kinds of selling? For example, if you're selling a highly technical product, do you just go to the customer and show them a catalog so they can place the order?"

Chuck realized that Jonathan was more experienced than he expected. He leaned back in his chair and in a less confrontational manner replied, "Yes, Jonathan, there are many kinds of sales. We sell a highly technical product that requires engineering expertise, familiarity with the solution selling that you mentioned, and they also need to be familiar with our internal processes so that the order can be properly placed and delivered, as ordered, on time."

"Great. Thanks, Chuck. Nathan, you've been quiet. Any thoughts?"

As Chuck and Jonathan were debating, Nathan was writing some notes on his pad. "I agree with Chuck and Brad - the brand is 'who we are'. But I'll get a bit more theoretical. I like to think of the brand as an image that people get when they hear the Company name 'Precision Technologies' – not only when they hear the words, but when they see any of our employees, talk to our employees, see one of our trucks. I'll take this well beyond seeing our name. It's not just a *thing*, but an expectation that we create with every interaction. It's not just our logo or words that we say."

Jonathan observed, "Interesting concept. Let's talk about interactions and expectations. Talk to me folks."

Nathan continued. "Chuck mentioned that we had a 1st class sales force. He also said well trained... technical. Can we say that about everyone in the Company? And if we say that, how do we measure 1st class? Compared to what? And does 1st class mean we process things properly, or do we just have a bunch of pretty faces in the Company?

You've got me on a roll, Jonathan. Interactions... are they always *perfect*? And what is perfect... measured how? "

"Wow, Nathan. Give me a minute to jot these things down." Jonathan enjoyed when the ideas were flowing so quickly that he couldn't keep up. He continued to write.

"Now, does 1st class mean the best ever? Made to NASA specs – nearest millionth of a centimeter – is that something like a billionth? Or does it mean give the customer what they need without overengineering?"

Brad responded, "Give the customers what they need."

"Ok does that mean if they don't ask for it, we don't give it to them? "

Brad responded, "No. We have well-trained, experienced engineers in the sales force, and we've got great resources here in the plant to help in unusual situations."

"Got it. Does that mean we like to partner with them to develop solutions to complex problems?"

Brad's immediate response. "From my side, I'd say yes. Chuck, Nathan, what do you think?"

Both nodded, agreement.

Jonathan jumped in immediately. "We've got agreement on the partnering aspect of our operation. Great. What *specifically* are we doing to promote that feature?"

Brad continued to look at Jonathan with a puzzled expression. Nathan and Chuck stared at each other.

"Well, we're working incredibly hard, Jonathan."

"Specifically, what are we doing to form that partnership mentality?"

BRAND

```
Products        Sales force  (1st class)
 - 1st class     - talented        -Employees
                 - well trained    -trucks
                   - technical     -interactions
                   - sales process -logo
                   - solution sale
                   -                        -processes
                                            -measures
                                            -training
                                            -expectations
      partnering                  -processes
                                     -Identify
                                     -Prioritize
                                   -Functions
                                     -Identify
                                     -Prioritize
```

After a minute Jonathan continued. "OK, brand is more of an all-encompassing idea that touches every process, every function, every person and interaction that the Company is involved with. We like the idea of thinking of ourselves as 1st class, but at this point we haven't specifically defined what it is or how we can achieve 1st class, or how we're going to get there. That's not a problem." He enthusiastically added, "This is a great start. Let's talk about the *market*. What is our market – and when I ask that questions, I'd like to understand who and what are our competitors. Thoughts?"

Competitors & Market

Nathan was quick to respond. "We compete against other high-tech industrial and precision measurement products."

"Great – in the state… the country or globally?"

"We'll accept an order from anywhere."

"I like the enthusiasm, Nathan. Does mean that we compete globally?"

Chuck added, "Nathan we generally sell within a 500-mile radius. We can't afford reps beyond that limit – 1 day's drive. Except we have a rep in Texas - more of a semi-rep – a retiree."

"And do, for example, German companies sell to customers within 500 miles?

Chuck puzzled for a moment. "I… I guess we have a global competitor locally."

Jonathan started to sketch on the whiteboard. "What do you think this is?"

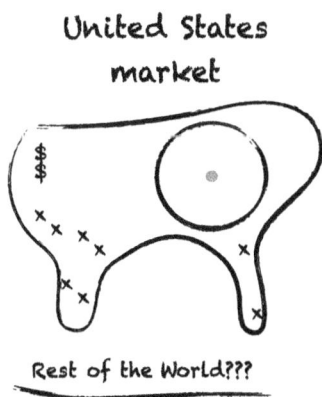

United States
market

Rest of the World???

"Profile of a headless Guernsey?"

"Thanks, Chuck. Not even close. Maybe I should skip the art work, but that is a map of the United States with a 500-mile circle around Cincinnati."

Chuck laughed. "Speaking of professional training, maybe we should volunteer some art lessons for you Jonathan."

Jonathan was now very pleased that Chuck was an active participant. "Ya got me, Chuck! Now I've got the 500-mile circle drawn, and our plan is to avoid selling outside the circle, right?"

"I wouldn't say avoid selling." Chuck was now on his feet, walking toward the whiteboard. He selected a marker, and placed a series of x's on the map of the US. "We've also sold in Texas, California, Arizona, Georgia and Florida."

"Great – how did those orders come in?"

"Those customers chased us … well, actually executives in companies that we sell to in the 500-mile radius moved on to other companies, and the relocated executive continued to purchase."

"And why?"

"Service – we helped them through some tough times with some of their engineering challenges in their previous companies."

"That would be the 'partnership' selling that we discussed earlier?"

Chuck agreed.

"Within the 500-mile circle where we compete, who are our competitors?"

Chuck started to list the names of competitors, as Jonathan scribed.

United States market

Rest of the World???

Competitors
* Alan Bradley
* HP
* United Tech
& Chelmsfor Ltd.
* Thor Industries
* LCI
& Jameson & Sons
* Lear
* Lennox
* Toledo
+ = large
& = small

"Looks like big & small, Chuck. What's a Clelmsfor?

"It's a British Company."

"And what's a Jameson?"

"Mom & pop in the Michigan area."

"I see a lot of big companies in your list. Do we compete the same with all the companies?"

Chuck continued to respond. "Big companies have deep pockets. It almost impossible to beat them on price per piece, but when we get in a tight relationship with the customer, they know we have that added-value approach."

"That's the partnering mentality that we talked about earlier?" Chuck agreed. "Do we use that partnering orientation on all sales calls?"

"No, we use it when we know that we're competing with the big guns. Otherwise, we just sell to the customers."

"And when we compete with the Chelmsfor and Jameson folks?"

"Chelmsfor is a Canadian company. Chelmsfor and Jameson are both Mom & Pops, so we don't get overly concerned about them. Usually they sell to smaller customers – below the radar. When we lose an order to them, it is not as big an impact."

"Ahah. Question. Have we defined an overall pricing strategy? Maybe by product line, or perhaps for the whole Company? "

Brad responded, "So far we've let the 'sales response team' - that's Chuck and the CFO - manage pricing, unless it really gets hairy. I get involved with very unusual pricing requirements."

"OK, let's keep poking at things."

Nathan offered, "Hold on, Chuck. Isn't Chelmsfor the company with the PhD owner that can turn an alarm clock into Spacelab-2? … kills us with mind-bending technology?"

"Yes, he's the thorn in my butt. When we compete against him, at best we break even, but sometimes we just don't want to lose a customer."

"Nathan, I've listened to a few items in the competitive discussion. Can we talk about the competitive strengths and weaknesses? Do we have a profile about our main competitors? Or maybe, do we have any analysis about the groups of competitors? For example, the small competitors and the global competitors?"

"Not yet, Jonathan. We've been working on so many other priorities."

"I understand. These days, there are 100 things to do every day. Do we have any idea about our current market share?"

"We don't have the money to spend on market research, Jonathan. We've joined one trade association and have a broad understanding of where we stand, but specifically, we don't have it."

"OK, as I understand the 2 main product lines, we have some electronic products, and some precision engineered metal castings. 'bout right?"

"Right on, Jonathan."

"When we review the industry statistics, do we have small, medium or large share in the lines?"

"We're small in each major segment."

"Let me draw a US market circle, and a global market circle for each. What's our guess?"

During the next few minutes, the team debated market sizes as Jonathan sketched – and modified – market share segments on the white board.

"Is this what we're thinking?"

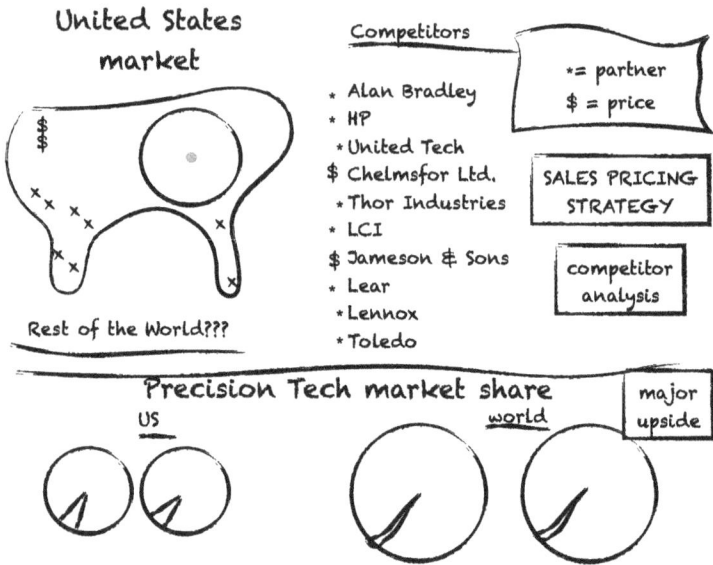

United States market

Competitors
* Alan Bradley
* HP
* United Tech
$ Chelmsfor Ltd.
* Thor Industries
* LCI
$ Jameson & Sons
* Lear
* Lennox
* Toledo

* = partner
$ = price

SALES PRICING STRATEGY

competitor analysis

Rest of the World???

Precision Tech market share

US

world

major upside

Jonathan let the team think about the information on the whiteboard.

Brad mused, "It looks like we have a lot of opportunity both in the states and in the world. … how do we get that share?"

Jonathan asked, "Brad, we didn't hear what you said."

"I said it looks like a helluva an opportunity. One boatload of opportunity."

Jonathan probed, "Something that you'd like to leave a mark on, Brad?"

Brad smiled.

"Let's summarize.

- We've got a great concept about our brand, but we haven't officially defined it – we manage the brand informally.
- Our brand image is affected by everything that we do and say.
- We compete with both large and small companies using 'partnering' and sometimes just pricing.
- Although we don't have a strict pricing strategy, we manage pricing through the pricing committee.
- We sell/promote within 500 miles of Cincinnati, except where we have executives from former customers who have migrated to other regions.
- On a worldwide basis, we have more than 95% market opportunity."

Nathan added, "And we have 95+% market opportunity here in the US."

All nodded in agreement.

Product

"Let's spend a few minutes on our products. We have two lines – electronics and precision castings, right?"

"Agreed" spoken in unison.

"Two things that interest me... age of the product lines, and our new product development pipeline."

Brad became uneasy – fidgeting in his seat. "Jonathan, I don't have a lot of money to spend on new product development. And to be fair, I haven't pushed the engineers for a lot of new products. We get along, as I've told you before."

"Is it fair to say that we don't have a good idea about the age of our products?"

"Not that we don't have an idea. Let's just say our sales are concentrated in a legacy product line, rather than too many new products. When a customer needs a new product, we work with them to develop one – I'll call it *development on demand*."

Jonathan added, "That's where a lot of our customer responsiveness high grades come from?

OK, let's keep going. When we get a call from the customer, do we see any trends in their requests?"

Chuck immediately responded, "You bet. They're looking for smaller circuitry to cut down on machine real estate, reduce power consumption, and improve reliability."

"Any others?"

"That's it 90% of the time."

"And when we lose an order to a competitor, is it possible that it is because of our outdated circuitry?"

Brad looked down at the table and didn't respond.

Jonathan knew this was a sore topic. "Let's continue. Earlier we mentioned that we sometimes need to drop our price to compete. Any thoughts?"

"Given the age of some of our electronic products, we have to give up some margin."

"Thanks, Nathan. Let's play on the board."

For the next few minutes they used theoretical examples of some of the existing product's approximate sales and margins. They added several new products, speculated about some gross margin rates, and discussed potential products that might be worthwhile in the marketplace.

Hypothetical

	Today	Tomorrow
Sales		
Prod A	25	25
Prod B	10	10
Prod C	20	20
Prod d	25	25
New Prod 1	–	10
New Prod 2	–	20
Total	80	110
Gross Margin		
Prod A	12	12
Prod B	4	4
Prod C	8	8
Prod d	10	10
New Prod 1		6
New Prod 2		13
Total	34	53
% of Sales	43%	48%

Jonathan continued. "I know that we've been making up these numbers – they are not real - but based on your market knowledge, do these concepts hang together? Not precise accounting numbers, but realistic?"

Not waiting for a response, Jonathan continued.

"This quick summary shows that we could conceivably increase our sales by up to $30 million and gross profit by

$19 million… and our gross margin rate by 5%. Good or bad?"

Brad became somewhat defensive. "C'mon Jonathan, we've just created these numbers on the fly."

"I hear you Brad. If we don't think they're reasonable, let's change them. Just for the heck of it, let's drop them by 10% - no let's make it 20%. So now we have an additional $15 million of gross profit. Two questions for you:

1. How much will it cost us to develop the products?
2. How much incremental selling cost will we have?"

Nathan challenged Jonathan. "I think we're in the ozone making up numbers, Jonathan. Too much speculation."

"Let's say we're off by 50%. Do you think that's possible?"

Hypothetical

Sales	Today	Max	Tomorrow Less 10%	20%	50%
Prod A	25	25	25	25	25
Prod B	10	10	10	10	10
Prod C	20	20	20	20	20
Prod d	25	25	25	25	25
New Prod 1	-	10	9	8	5
New Prod 2	-	20	18	16	10
Total	80	110	107	104	95
Gross Margin					
Prod A	12	12	12	12	12
Prod B	4	4	4	4	4
Prod C	8	8	8	8	8
Prod d	10	10	10	10	10
New Prod 1		6	5	5	6
New Prod 2		13	11	10	6
Total	34	53	50	49	46
% of Sales	43%	48%	47%	47%	48%

"Maybe."

"Now I'm down to an extra $12million incremental gross margin. What will the incremental selling costs total?"

"Just commissions…we already call on the customers."

"Will new products help us get more customers? Remember that 95% market opportunity here in the US?"

Chuck stood and walked to the board. "And the rest of the world. I could really use the new products to crack open some new markets and get some new local customers."

"Do we have an upside on two fronts?"

"Agreed," in unison.

"Let's focus on today's product portfolio. Do we have any tired products that clutter our catalog?"

Brad thought about our products. "Sure, we have some tired products, but why would we not accept an order if we have the products in house?"

Jonathan smiled. "Two reasons. 1. It costs money to stock parts and 2. When a part supply gets low, do we reorder? And if we reorder, will there be any minimum order or price premium?

I'm not suggesting that we just get rid of old products, but I am suggesting that we evaluate their true value and cost to the Company. We might find some surprises when the analysis in done.

Product pruning may be valuable… shall we move on?"

Jonathan continued. "This has been an excellent discussion so far, but I think it's time for us to take a break. It's 10:15. Let's regroup at 10:30. We'll start to discuss the marketing mix."

Chuck adjourned to the rest room – far too much coffee this early in the day.

Brad and Nathan huddled while considering either the Danish or the bagel with cream cheese.

"So, what do you think, Nathan?"

"I was a bit skeptical about spending a day with an outsider – especially someone from outside the industry. … not sure what was to be gained. But the last two hours have given me a lot to think about. On the one side, it's refreshing to think about our business in ways other than today's budget and P&L.

He's asking some difficult questions… not sure if we should know the answers, but it sure makes me think about opportunities I hadn't considered before. You?"

Brad selected the raspberry Danish. "… going off my diet – but since we're talking about change, why not just leap from the current diet and enjoy the event."

Brad paused, thinking about the morning. "I guess you've seen that I don't agree with some of his statements, but … well it's clear that he's a better businessman than golfer."

Brad was noncommittal about his assessment of our guest.

Chuck returned to the conference room and immediately moved to the refreshments. He looked directly at Brad. "What do you think?"

"I think that he's a better businessman than golfer..." repeating the same observation as with Nathan.

"You can do better than that, Brad. I know your expressions, and you've been unhappy about a few things said. What do you really think?"

"I think that Jonathan is asking a lot of questions. I'm not quite sure whether this is purely an academic exercise, or an entre' into a more meaningful analysis that helps us become a more valuable Company. But for the sake of a day's investment, I'm all for it."

Brad did not want to discount the day's efforts, since he trusted Jonathan to provide value.

At 10:30, Jonathan reconvened the session.

"Let's talk about the marketing mix. Any thoughts about what that might include?"

"I'm guessing that it's a discussion about our advertising and promotion programs, our collateral material, trade shows etc."

"Great start, Nathan. But let me ask a broader question. How do we interact with actual and potential customers, deal with the competitive, legal, and regulatory environment?

We've touched on brand, customers and product. How do we make the Company more successful?"

Brad leaned forward at the conference table. "When you ask the question that broadly, are you really asking about our resources going outside the four walls?"

"Excellent. Yes, but not only going outside the four walls, but observations coming into our business.

Let's back up a bit. In its purest sense, the entire Company should be aligned to improving the Company value. When I think about the whole Company, I like to consider every interaction we have - anywhere, anytime - as part of the *marketing mix*."

Chuck objected. "I'd like to call a *BS* on you, Jonathan. Marketing is what Nathan does. Not sales… not manufacturing … not administration, HR, finance, legal etc. The so-called *marketing mix* is Nathan's to manage."

"Thanks for the pushback, Chuck. I may be getting a bit too theoretical, but when I think of a Company in a highly competitive environment, every action that we take can have an impact on our performance. I'll exaggerate. If we have a poorly trained sales rep, will that have an impact on sales?"

"Of course. But sales are my game, Jonathan. It could have an impact on sales, but that's my problem, not Nathan's."

"If Nathan is responsible for managing the brand, is a well-trained sales rep part of our *brand* image?"

"Sure, that's what we defined earlier. But it's still my turf."

"Let me continue. If we have a poorly designed website, that is not responsive to customers and potential customers, is that potentially part of our brand?"

"Sure, because we're dealing with customers. But that responsibility is owned by our IT director. That's not Nathan's job."

"And one last item. If the finance folks are difficult to deal with – overly aggressive or maybe too restrictive with credit - is that part of our brand?"

Chuck, becoming less forceful in his dispute, said, "Well, yes, it's part of our brand. But what the hell does that have to do with the marketing mix?"

"OK. My point is that just because we call something a 'marketing mix' doesn't mean it only applies to Nathan. There are many attributes to the brand. We discussed many of them earlier.

The Marketing Mix will include all those elements that relate directly to actual and potential customers. When you read the text books, marketing includes four elements: Product, Price, Promotion and Place.

I'd like to spend a few minutes just brainstorming about things we do to influence our actual and potential customers. I've got the marker – make me work folks."

Nathan immediately responded with, "… brochures, advertising, technical white papers, trade shows, community relations…"

Chuck tried several times to break into the discussion, and finally stood up and said, "sales reps, manufacturer's reps, commissions, travel & entertainment...."

Brad added, "... community relations, contributions, support of the little league, trade association memberships & leadership positions..."

They each continued to add topics as Jonathan encouraged them to make him work. The pace quickened for about 10 minutes, and then the feedback slowed.

Jonathan flipped the marker in the air, and as he caught the marker, said I've got two tickets to the Sunday Reds game for the one that gives the most suggestions in the next 3 minutes.

Chuck immediately volunteered, "TV and Radio advertising, print media, web site, sales salaries, SPIFS, in-house phone sales, distributors, Joint Ventures."

Once Jonathan wrote the last suggestions, he smiled broadly and said, "Bribes work Chuck. 3rd row behind the Red's bench. You'll have a great time, but the beers are on you.

And now we have somewhat of a comprehensive list of STUFF that we might consider to be part of the marketing mix. There may be some others, but for now, let me just jiggle the info around for a few minutes. Shall we take 10 minutes so that you can catch up with your email and voicemails?"

brochures	community relations
advertising	contributions
technical white papers	little league
trade shows	trade association
community relations	- memberships
sales reps	- leadership
manufacturer reps	- board meemberships
commissions	seasonal themes
t&e	mailings
new products	keyword analysis
new product launch	apprenticeships
university relations	website
catalogs	sales salary
advertising	SPIFS
- web	In-house Phone sales
- print media	distributors, JV's
	product pipeline

He turned to the whiteboard, took a picture, and began to summarize in a different way.

After 10 minutes, the team returned to find a new chart on the whiteboard.

Brainstorming – Marketing Mix	Sales	Mkting	IT	R&D	HR
Sales Reps					
–Sales Salary	X				
–Commissions	X				
–SPIFS	X				
–T&E	X				
In-house sales	X				
Manufacturer Reps	X				
Distributors	X				
JV's	X				
Brochures		X			
Catalogs		X			
Mailings		X			
Advertising		X			
– web		X			
–Print Media		X			
Website	X	X	X	X	X
keyword analysis		X			
New Products	X	X		X	
New Product launch		X			
Product Pipeline		X		X	
Seasonal/cyclical themes	X	X		X	
trade association					
– memberships	X	X		X	
– leadership	X	X		X	
– board meemberships	X	X		X	
trade shows	X	X		X	
technical white papers				X	
community relations					X
little league					X
contributions					X
apprenticeships					X

"Let's review this updated chart. I've adjusted the original list – looking for some feedback. Earlier, we listed – oh, maybe 20 items – that could be considered part of our marketing mix… the things that could influence customers to work with us. Some of them – well, you can see that they are a direct relationship to getting the customer order. Others, may be indirectly related, but they all impact *brand*. Now, we're not here today to develop any kind of a spending plan, but I want to expose the concept that a marketing mix means a lot of things. It's not just assembling some brochures to distribute at a trade show. Spend a few minutes and look at this and let's discuss the chart."

Brad observed, "Your website line has an 'X' in sales, marketing, IT, R&D, and HR. What's that about?"

"That's a great question, Brad. Firstly, we know why IT has an "X". The IT folks are technical experts – they can prepare a website. But I think that we want the Website to serve several functions… tell the outside world about the Company… the products and markets that we sell to … perhaps directionally where our new product strategy will take us… help us launch new products… maybe have informative videos or white-papers discussing the products and upcoming technology. I'd like to think that part of the mix might be with Human Resources. Maybe for recruiting purposes, or perhaps to convey our community orientation.

You might not consider these to be priorities, but when you think of outbound communications, what is a better medium than an up-to-date website? Thoughts?"

Brad scowled slightly. "…might be a bit of a stretch, but I get it. "

Nathan stood up and walked to the board. "I think that the 'keyword' analysis doesn't capture everything that we intend to do. I sure as heck would like to understand what our competitors are doing. You know, maybe have some kind of competitive assessment. I've heard that there is a keyword search where we can automatically get notification when a company name is mentioned in the news."

"Great suggestion, Nathan."

Chuck injected, "Now that you mention keyword search, how about a process where we scan the press for news about our clients. I'd like to hear immediately if one of my clients gets a big contract, or maybe makes a critical hire. I'd show them some love with a quick email of congrats. Is that keyword thing easily done?"

"I think it takes minutes, but let's not solve all the issues now – let's just list them. Other comments?"

Brad offered, "I don't see anything on that list for customer feedback or maybe survey results. As long as we're listing *everything*, let's add it. But I'll caution everyone – it seems like we're spending a lot of money..." ... Brad's voice trailed off.

"No worries, Brad. I just wanted to get a full population of what we think might be part of the mix." Jonathan continued, "Now comes the self-analysis. We've identified what might be the marketing mix for the Company, and now I want you to think about how we perform each of these activities."

Nathan, without comment, stared at the extensive list and doodled on the yellow pad.

Chuck self-consciously picked at the paper cup, tearing small strips from the rim.

Brad stared intently at the list, and then spoke. "I'll speak for the Company. That's a hell of a list. We haven't ever thought about our business in those terms – I guess because we've been successful for many years. I like the creativity and understand how it might help us be more profitable, but it looks like a lot of money to be spent. I don't really have an answer to the question."

Jonathan sensed the negative emotion – almost defeatist. "Wait a minute, Brad. You've been successful for the past 20 years. This is a brainstorming session. Perhaps many of the topics we discussed can't be implemented immediately, but I can tell you that at other companies, many of these items can be implemented without extra cost.

The point of the exercise is to identify the population of possible sales & marketing activities, and not to say we can or can't implement them. That's for another time. I can tell you that the work that we've done this morning tells me that you are creative and have many ideas that can be implemented.

It's a long list – I agree. And you may not be doing some of these things as thoroughly as you'd like. But if we take the next step – perhaps a deeper dive into the individual topics - we might find that we can start some new activities, increase sales and increase the resources available for investment.

Hey, it's lunchtime. Brad, did you order food, or will we be roasting steaks on the Barbie?"

"Panera is ready to go, so let's have lunch. Jonathan, got a minute."

Chuck and Nathan selected their sandwiches as Brad and Jonathan huddled.

"Jonathan, can you be straight with me. Are we a mess or what?"

"Not at all, Brad. I meant to shake things a bit today, but just based on this morning's efforts, I can sense a great opportunity. If we take the next step of more in-depth analysis, I think that you'll find a tremendous upside to your normal business trends.

The key to this kind of assessment and planning activity is to think without constraints. Let's get the creative opportunities on the table, and then decide how we prioritize, and then execute the program. You feel a bit exposed now because so many great ideas surfaced. The next step is to prioritize the opportunities and then execute those that we can afford.

We will cover sales this afternoon. That should be very interesting considering our work this morning. Let's grab a sandwich."

For the next half-hour, small-talk dominated the lunch discussion. Jonathan made some notes about how to approach the afternoon session.

Jonathan snapped a picture and cleaned the board to remove all remnants of the morning's work.

"And so, we start fresh. Everybody enjoy the Panera lunch?"

"Excellent lunch. It's always nice if it tastes good and is healthy as well."

Chuck laughed. "You young folks – always looking for healthy. Sure, it was good, but you can't beat a basket of Buffalo Wild Wings with Mango Habanero sauce. While we're talking, make it 2 dozen wings, Jonathan."

They all laughed at Chuck's dietary preferences. Brad added, "And don't forget a side order of Prilosec, Chuck."

Jonathan knew that when a team was joking about some personal habits, the team would be very productive.

"This afternoon, Chuck will be the highlight. We're going to be talking about sales, the sales organization and the selling process. We all on board with that?"

"If I can't get my 2 dozen wings, I won't have enough energy to finish the afternoon."

Nathan said, "Not to worry, Chuck. I've got a half-pint of your favorite hot-sauce on order, just in case your energy wanes."

"Let's start with the sales function. Let's start with a general discussion about how we perform 'sales.

Sales Rep – Time Spent

"Let's just do a data dump. What is our sales organization? I'd like us all to pitch in to this conversation with any comments that you like, and I'll scratch on the whiteboard."

"I think I'm picking up a whiteboard pattern here, Jonathan." Smiling, Chuck continued, "I have 5 sales reps scattered across the country, and I have one customer service operator that handles the reps panic calls.

I also have two manufacturer's reps in the Pacific Northwest."

"And what does a rep do all day?"

"We expect them to make an average of 4 sales calls a day when they're on the road."

"And how often are they on the road?"

"Maybe 60% of the time."

"What do they do with the other 40%?"

Nathan jumped into the conversation. "We spend quite a bit of time with the reps responding to questions about developing proposals for some of the bigger orders. Sometimes we talk with them about new product developments."

"And how does that come about?"

"Most times it is in response to a competitor's new product launch. The rep calls a meeting with Chuck, me and Randy, the VP engineering."

"Sounds good. Where else does the rep spend time?"

"They spend time arranging their trips, coordinating schedules with clients. They also do some trade research–business trends, maybe the impact of foreign competitors… They might also work on some special contract negotiations."

"Sounds good. And what time allocation among actual and potential clients? Anything specific?"

"No, we let them determine how they manage their individual territories."

"And do we provide guidelines for their time allocation between actual and potential?"

Chuck was beginning to get concerned about the direction of the questions. "You're getting into the weeds, Jonathan."

Jonathan persisted, "So is it 80/20 actual to potential? You're right, that might be too much into the weeds." Jonathan wanted to leave a number hanging as he continued to press on with the activities.

All the while he was asking the questions, Jonathan was scratching things on the white board.

Sales Reps Time

Rep	Hunt/ Farm	Road Work	Home Office	Ans ??	Cmplaint	Proposals	New Prod	Trav Plan
			Home Office					
1		60%	40%					
2		60%	40%					
3		60%	40%					
4		60%	40%					
5		60%	40%					

"And how much time do we spend on 'A' accounts versus 'C 'accounts?"

"Again, Jonathan, we leave the time allocation up to the reps."

"Got it. Have we reviewed our customer turnover statistics? Do you know, how many we lose each year? And the reasons we lost them? And how about the number of lost bids that we've produced, and the reasons that we lost the bid?"

"Whoa bronco. You're moving far too fast. We're a small Company, and we don't have the resources to do all that analysis."

"Gotcha. How many trade shows do we attend each year?"

"We do four a year. East & West, spring and fall."

"And how is our lead tracking? Have we found that the trade shows are extremely successful, somewhat successful?"

"We've had great luck with the shows. Sales are up every year."

"Ah, but you didn't answer my question about lead tracking. If we were to complete a trade show summary like this each time, what would it show?"

Trade Show results

Call Cycle:			Spring		Fall	
			East	West	East	West
A	18 months?					
B	6 months?	$ Sales				
c	days??	# Leads				
		a				
		b				
		c				

Trade Show Booth

"Do you think we should do anything differently?"

"Our booth is shabby. We could use a new, more modern setup. Some of our competitors have some videos with their R&D execs explaining why their products are superior. But we've got some excellent brochures – not the same sizzle, though."

"And as long as we're just brainstorming, some iPads for the reps might make things a lot simpler to do business."

Chuck added, "I'm not sure that we're competitive in our compensation. We've lost a few reps during the past few years... I think it was the comp."

"Are your reps hunters or farmers?"

"Each rep is multi-purpose. They hunt and farm. Maybe not the best approach, but we can't afford the high potential hunters."

"If sales were to increase by 15%, what kind of additional profit would you have for comp?"

Brad leaned forward, "We can't afford higher compensation. Period."

"OK, Brad. I've got that note. Let's keep going. Do we use webinars for sales promotion?"

"Jonathan, we are a straightforward sales force. We travel to the clients and sell. No webinars"

Santa Brainstorming

"Let me ask the question another way. If you could do anything you want – Santa Claus comes to town and will give you anything you want, what would you wish for, Chuck?"

Jonathan looked at Brad – smiled & winked as if to assure him the exercise would be worthwhile.

Chuck stood up and started pacing, while rattling off a series of improvements that Jonathan could hardly keep up with him.

Santa's Wish List

- New computers
- salesforce.com
- better commission plan
- mileage allowance
- additional clerk
- better brochures
- better SWAG
- entertainment $
- distributors
- add a rep
- new products
- competitive info pipeline
- memberships
- cycle of stuff
- engineer visits to clients
- speaking opportunities
- interns

- sales training
- a hunter on staff
- beter communications
- pricing flexibility
- broader product line
- gov't contracting expert
  - fed
  - muni
- international
  - canada
  - europe
  - brazil
- foreign language website
- website videos
- webinars
- tech white papers

After 5 minutes, Chuck grinned at Jonathan, and said, "How'd I do, Santa?"

Brad, shocked at the length of the list, looked surprised and said, "Wow!" … and not another word.

Jonathan responded to Chuck. "Well Dr. Chuck, I'd say that we uncorked a gusher. This is an extraordinary ad hoc list. … glad Santa came to town. Have a few of these things been waiting for the right opportunity to launch?"

"You might say so. And these are off the top of my head. There may be others. Is this the only Santa list I can prepare?"

"I think we want to get all the opportunities on the table, all the time. I don't think that we should wait for Santa to show up. The beauty of this Santa exercise is... well let me ask a question. Did we just spend any money creating this list?"

"Not yet," Brad quickly responded.

"If we didn't spend any money, what have we accomplished?"

"Looks like a brain dump of frustration to me," Nathan suggested.

"Not at all. This is a preliminary list of opportunity to improve the business. I've got this theory that everybody has 5-10% of time that can be redeployed to more valuable activity. So, let's take today as an example. We've taken 1 day from each of your schedules. If we have a 200-day year, we've dedicated a half-percent of your time to identify perhaps 50 actionable tasks that may improve the future of the Company.

The next step might be to evaluate the items... prioritize them based on their tactical and strategic value to the Company, then develop and execute a plan to reap the benefits. Thoughts?"

"Does this mean that we're done with the sales portion?"

"Not yet, Chuck."

"OK, my thoughts are that this has been refreshing and I agree with your math. A half-percent is a nit."

After a minute of silence, Jonathan continued, "So let's proceed. For the past 2 hours we've talked about the sales function. That would be how we directly interact with the actual and potential customers, to get a sale. We've talked about how we have our representatives help customers identify their needs, and we satisfy their needs.

Now let's look at the whiteboard that we've been developing."

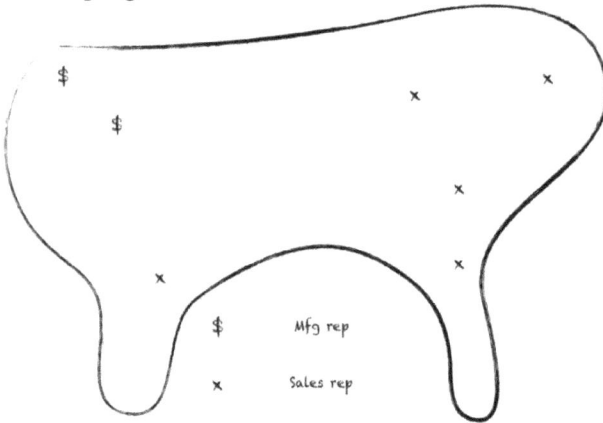

$
$
x
x
x
x
x
$ Mfg rep
x   Sales rep

"There's that weird Guernsey again, Jonathan. Makes me want to drive to Chick-Fil-A."

Pausing briefly for effect, Jonathan then said, "I have the copyright on the design and the monthly royalty checks are outstanding....

You know, it does make me think of a Chicken Sandwich."

Sales Rep – Productive Time

"But to get back to the topic, as Chuck was speaking earlier, I was writing notes. I've just circled some of the main ideas or concepts that we were exploring. Any comments, Chuck?"

Rep	Hunt Farm	Road Work	Home Office	Ans ??	Complaints	Home Office Proposals	New Prod	Trav Plan
				Sales Reps Time				
1		60%	40%	10%		20%	5%	5%
2		60%	40%	10%		20%	5%	5%
3		60%	40%	10%		20%	5%	5%
4		60%	40%	10%		20%	5%	5%
5		60%	40%	10%		20%	5%	5%

"Yes, the first thing I noticed is that you have put percentages in the Home Office portion of the sales reps matrix. I don't remember giving you the numbers."

Jonathan often developed a straw man when he brainstormed with any team. He found it worthwhile to speculate about some of the values to challenge people's thinking.

"Great question, Chuck. I like to put some placeholders in the analysis. It helps frame the scale for folks. For example, I wouldn't want to get hung up on any concentration of effort less than 5%. But the numbers I've put in are definitely mine. Any thoughts from you and the team?"

"Does that 5% mean 5% of their total time? Or is it 5% of the 'Home' time?"

"It's 5% of their total time. On average, the rep spends 2 hours a week on travel logistics. Does that sound right?"

"Well, it's not stupid. I guess it makes sense. And why would you put 10% in answers & complaints?"

"Again, we're talking about an average of 4 hours a week. I made the number up. And I did the same with the 20% of proposal time. Here's what I'd like us to think about. We pay a lot for a trained rep. When I think of their valuable time, and I think of road work plus home office time, I'd like to discover exactly how much face time they spend with the customer.

If a rep averages 3 days a week out of the office – that would be the 60% - how much of that time is actually in front of the customer? Could it be as little as 3-4 hours a day? 3-4 calls a day, with the rest being wait time, windshield and airport time?

Ideally, they get paid for being in front of the customer. When we actually take a survey, we may find that out of a normal workweek, they may only spend 20 hours a week in the selling mode. Would that be good or bad?"

"If we're paying for 40 hours a week of a trained sales rep, that basically doubles their productive time cost. But given the constraints of travel, I'm not sure how to fix that."

"We're not going to answer that here, but if we were to carefully analyze their time, and could find 3+- hours a week of - I'll call it facetime with the customer – that 3 hours a week is a 15% productivity improvement. And we didn't spend a nickel extra."

"Great theory, Jonathan, but this is the real world. "

"I accept your challenge, Chuck. But let's just play *what if* for a few minutes. We're not going to solve the problem here, but let's just speculate.

When we say facetime with the client, what does that really mean?"

"It means that the rep sits down with the client to reinforce the business relationship, listens to their problems and business issues, talks about their needs and possible solutions. It means that they take the client out to dinner – change of venue – so that the formal business-to-business curtain comes down."

"And is that different if it's an existing client versus prospecting?"

"Sure. Sometimes it takes more time commitment to establish a working relationship with a prospect."

"Is part of that relationship just letting them know that we care about their business? Maybe it's also to get us above the radar line? Get our name in front of them?"

"That's definitely a piece."

"And is traveling to their site the only way to accomplish the 'above the radar', and let them know that we care?"

"I don't get it. That's what sales is."

"And do we think that they are waiting for our routine visit? Is it sometimes inconvenient to host us for a meeting? Do we intrude on their day?"

"I guess it could sometimes be an intrusion, but it's important that they think about us."

"Right. And is there more than one way for them to think about us? For example, if we were to have a meaningful white paper sent to them periodically, would that get us above the radar?"

"It might."

"OK let's take a different approach. If we could reduce their 'travel planning' from 2 hours a week average to 1 hour, would that give them more productive time?"

"Sure, but that's only 1 hour."

"And if we could free up another 2 hours by somehow having more standardization in our contract proposals – and I'm not sure how to do that – but would we then have created 3 hours a week to dedicate to face-time?

And when we have, for example, 2 hours a week handling customer complaints or questions, will we free up another 1-2 hours by searching for the root cause of the complaints and eliminate the problem."

Nathan perked up with that last statement. "You know, Chuck, we do have quite a few meetings with the reps trying to straighten out billing problems, design problems, timely shipping etc. There just may be 1-2 hours a week on average that could free up."

"Thanks Nathan. Chuck, I'm not saying any of these things will work, but if we don't know where their time is going, how can we say the time available isn't there? Let's pick on an easy one. Let's have an admin who handles all the travel arrangements. So now we definitely have traded a relatively high-cost rep's time for clerical cost. Thoughts?"

"I think it might be worthwhile to do some research, but I'm not making any commitments about time saved."

"Agreed. Now let's spend a few minutes focused on how we allocate time. Is it better or worse to spend time with 'A' actual/potential clients?"

Customer Profile
     #   Annual $
< 1 year
>1<2 year
2+ years

What's an A customer???

Customer Profile — $ Sales

	A		B		C	
	Act	Pot	Act	Pot	Act	Pot
# Accts						

How much time should we plan to spend on A vs. B vs. C?
How much time should we spend on Act vs.

"Of course, it's better to invest in 'A' clients."

"And if we could increase our time invested in 'A' clients without any incremental spending, is that a good thing?"

"Of course, it's a good thing."

"So how much time do our reps spend on 'A' clients today?"

"I'm not sure. Remember I said earlier that we leave that up to the reps."

"I understand. Do you think that there may be an opportunity to focus more energy on the *A's*?"

"I know what you're doing, Jonathan. It would be foolish for me to say no. The next thing you're going to tell me is that we should try to refocus on the *A's*, right?"

"As you've said, it would be foolish for me to say no. Look, Chuck, I'm not trying to box you into anything that doesn't make sense, because I don't know anything about your business. You are the expert. My role in business is to help folks identify the processes that will help them allocate scarce resources to get the greatest benefit.

You are always in charge."

During the discussion Brad was taking notes. He picked up his head, looked at Nathan and Chuck and said, "You know, these questions seem to make sense. Sometimes I think we need to pick up our heads and look around. Earlier I heard someone say we should have webinars. Well, we've never done that. Someone else said whitepapers would be helpful. Did I hear something about Google search words and sending notes to clients?

Well, we don't do any of those things, and first blush, it seems that they may be worthwhile. Comments?"

Nathan offered, "I'm with you Brad. We don't do any of those things. The question for you is how much can we afford?"

"Nathan, if we can crank up the sales dollars, we'll have some flexibility. I'm not saying that we can increase sales by thinking differently, but I'm willing to try."

Brad looked at Nathan and Chuck assessing what we thought we could afford to invest. "Thinking and whiteboarding doesn't cost us much. Today we've spent maybe 5 hours exploring areas that we've never considered, and we have fifty ideas. Some mean using existing resources, some need spending. Maybe if we pace things properly, we can fund these ventures. Maybe…"

Jonathan spoke. "That's exactly right Brad. It's an insignificant investment to explore strategies and activities that could – as you've said – 'leave a mark'. "

Staring intently at Jonathan, Brad asked, "What do you recommend as the next steps, Jonathan?"

"I'll guess at an approach. If I spent no more than 1-2 days each with the marketing and sales teams, I think that we would have specific activities outlined, including expected earnings impact.

In those meetings, we'd start with some of the things that we discussed today, and get more down in the weeds, to get more definitive information about next steps. I've been doing this for years, and I think that you'd be pleasantly surprised at the results. What do you think?"

Brad looked at Chuck and Nathan. "What do you folks think?"

"I'll block two days, but if it doesn't look beneficial, I'd like the opportunity to stop the review."

"That sounds fair, Nathan. Chuck, what do you think?"

"You want me to take my guys out of the field to do this exercise?"

"No, I want you to decide who should attend. Remember, we're data mining and we want to hear the information from the front lines. What do you think is best?"

"I'll have to noodle that a bit. But I think that the more in-depth analysis is worth a try."

"Brad, I'll put these notes together to give you the foundation. We don't need to make any commitments today, but I think this was a great day. We've challenged our way of doing business in sales & marketing. We've identified dozens of possible opportunities that may help you become a bigger, more profitable business.

You folks have done a great job by accepting the challenge and breaking through historical barriers." He smiled broadly, looking at Chuck. "I will admit it took Santa's wish list to get Chuck turbocharged, but this was a great session.

Thanks for all your help."

Brad dismissed the team, and spoke with Jonathan.

"What did you think of their participation?"

"This was a very successful day, Brad. I was a bit concerned initially about Chuck's receptiveness to an outsider telling him how to run his business, but he came around quickly when we got to Santa. … works every time.

Nathan seems to be on board. It may be due to his more recent marketing training, and maybe since he had less investment in Company history.

I think that if we follow through with this, you'll get your breakthrough results in both sales and marketing. What did you think of the day?"

"I was quite shocked at the number of things that popped up. I've been asking these folks, 'what should we do differently?' for years, and it's just crickets."

"Brad, that's not unusual. Think about it. You've held them accountable to budgets for years. They have ingrained constraints. They think, 'Oh, we can't spend that amount of money.' They haven't asked for more resources because they have always met their target without it.

Some companies routinely budget *last year plus inflation*. I like to push them by asking, 'how can we increase sales by 25%?' By asking the lofty goals question, I'm pushing them outside their historical constraints. It's surprising what pops up when you change the guard rails."

"OK, Jonathan. Thanks for your help today. I'll confirm our decision to move forward, and get back to you tomorrow."

They shook hands, and Jonathan took pictures of the whiteboard, cleared up his stack of papers, and left for the parking lot.

Brad stopped in Chuck's office for a debriefing.

"What did you think Chuck?"

"Now that was an interesting session. When you first mentioned an outside consultant, and then you said he was sometimes a golf partner, I was ready to head for the arctic. Think about it. The boss's friend – an old consultant. Jeeesh.

I expected a total waste of time. At first, the more he poked at us, the more uncomfortable I got. But then – I'm not sure why – but I got it. He was focused on what we do and how we do it. He wasn't telling us what to do. He was mining our experience, and challenging us for better ways. Heck, we both know that we haven't used some of the technology advantages available to us right now. Even something as simple as a webinar that we could deliver as early as tomorrow has never been on the radar.

I'm not going to commit to anything like a 25% increase in sales, but I will commit to more exploration and an open mind to more discussion with Jonathan."

"That's great, Chuck. Thanks for being so candid as we got into the discussion. I think I'll drop into Nathan's office. See you later."

Nathan was on the phone when Brad entered his office.

As he completed the call, Nathan looked at Brad. "How'd we do, boss?"

"No, Nathan, I get to ask the questions. What did you think of our time investment today? Worthwhile? Or not?"

"Today was time travel for me. Brought me back to my graduate courses in marketing theory. Back then, we had to learn the academic theory to pass the tests. Now, I'm in the real world and have a better idea of what that theory actually means. It's a bit embarrassing that I haven't really used the training in those grad courses.

Brad, I really enjoyed today's exercise. I'm not going to say that I can implement any of the things that we discussed this morning, but I will tell you I'm thinking a bit differently... I'll call it a more refreshing way to think about our business."

"So, will we do anything differently?"

"Good question. Today was a bit of rejuvenation for me. I've got a lot of new ideas, but I think we need a practical discussion about what can really be implemented, given real world constraints – money, people resources etc. But my gut tells me that I can definitely develop some very specific actions that will be implemented during the next 6 months.

Brad, are you on board with Jonathan's concepts?"

"I am if you and Chuck are in the game. I think that you and Chuck will have a list of actions that you'll want me to fund. And then it's up to me to either put-up or shut-up. And considering my desire to stir things up – I think that's perfect. I like the phrase that Jonathan used this morning…'Make me work…"

As Brad left Nathan's office, he was pleased that he invited Jonathan to this exploratory session. When he returned to his office, he sent Jonathan a note. "How about lunch tomorrow at the Mt. Adam's Bar & Grill to follow up on today's discussion? 11:45AM? …it gets very busy at lunch time."

Jonathan saw Brad's email pop up on his phone and immediately responded, "Sure – haven't been there in a while. Will be good to get reacquainted with the place. … a unique cultural oasis in the city. See you there."

Feedback Session – Jonathan & Brad

Jonathan arrived at 11:30 to enjoy the iconic restaurant. 'The Grill,' as many referred to the restaurant, was one of the first bars in Ohio to serve alcohol after prohibition's repeal. In 1920, it may have also been one of the first to serve illicit alcohol when prohibition was enacted.

As he looked around the restaurant, he thought, '*The owners have developed a unique environment with 'the president's wall – autographed original pictures from several presidents – and several other unique memorabilia including an autographed poster of John Glenn.*

The décor was a blend of traditional neighborhood pub, and an eclectic collection of exotic things from the Jackaroo to an elk's head mounted trophy, to model trains scattered along the top rail along the bar.

The bar reportedly is an original artifact from a 19th century Chicago hotel. … very interesting.

Jonathan selected a booth so that they had enough space to work, and also enjoy some privacy during their conversation.

Shortly after he was seated, Brad entered.

A quick wave, and Brad joined him.

"Hey, you got here early, Jonathan."

"Yes, it's been a while since I've been here and I wanted to reacquaint myself with the ambiance. Now I understand why this is on the 'most visited' places in Cincinnati."

"Gets even better. The 'Blind Lemon' next door has an equally unique environment. I think that between the two establishments, there isn't a married couple from Cincinnati that hasn't sipped a cocktail at one of them."

The waitress arrived with the menu's and they quickly ordered lunch.

"So now the tough part is over, Jonathan. I've talked with Chuck and Nathan, and they think it might be worthwhile to spend some more time with you. I tend to agree with them, since in only a few hours we identified many areas for improvement. I'm not convinced how much I can afford, but I can certainly afford to spend a few more days with you on Marketing and Selling. Are you open for more discussion? Or maybe I should say, 'What do you suggest?"

"First, let me say that you and your team did a wonderful job brainstorming. Chuck and Nathan were a bit skeptical at first, but once we got into the topics, we really accomplished a lot… probably in the top 10% performance in all the interventions that I've coordinated.

I've been thinking of next steps after your initial feedback, and I'd suggest a whole day each on marketing and selling. These will be open discussion about 'what could be' given your Company's market position, current and potential resources.

We'd dig more deeply into each subtopic. For example, in the marketing segment, we'd include branding, communications (inbound and outbound), competitive discussion, new product development and product pruning, marketing mix etc. In the selling area, we'd cover selling strategy, ranking customers (A-B-C), prioritization of sales efforts, composition of sales force (hunters and farmers), new product development, CRM applications etc.

I think that if we spent no more than a day in each area, we'd have an executable plan that would improve your business. Thoughts?"

"It's a simple decision for me. I've got a hundred-million-dollar Company. For the sake of two days effort, I see no downside to spending a few more dollars to identify opportunity to protect and grow this business. I'm going to look at your efforts as if you're a profit center, not a cost center. I'll have Tracey schedule the time.

And now let's enjoy lunch."

Brad changed topics to the upcoming club tournament and his expectations.

During the next few days, Tracey scheduled one day each for Nathan and Chuck to brainstorm with Jonathan. At

Jonathan's suggestion, she also requested that the marketing staff and sales reps attend their respective sessions, if it fit their schedules. This was not a mandatory meeting.

MARKETING & SALES DISCUSSION

Nathan & Marketing Staff Meet with Jonathan

Jonathan opened the meeting.

"Welcome Nathan. I'm glad that your staff was able to join us today. This will be a very productive session where we explore opportunities in marketing. I'll label this a brainstorming session, which means there are no bad comments. If something is on your mind, we want to hear about it.

Let's start with the definition of marketing, compliments of Merriam Webster:

"… the process or technique of promoting, selling, and distributing a product or service.
… an aggregate of functions involved in moving goods from producer to consumer."

Any thoughts about the definition?"

The marketing team included Emily, an analyst, and Allie, administrative support. Nathan was familiar with the definition, but Emily and Allie seemed puzzled.

Jonathan allowed a few seconds for questions, and then asked, "Are you comfortable with these definitions, ladies?"

Allie sipped her coffee, while Emily cleared her throat, ready to speak. But she remained silent.

"Emily, looks like you're ready to pop with a question. Don't be shy – let's hear it."

"Well, I see the words promoting, selling and distributing. And the definition also talks about functions moving goods from producer to consumer. That's not what we do in marketing."

Jonathan was extremely pleased at Emily's observation. "Well, let's spend a minute on the definition. Are you comfortable that the Company's objective is to promote, sell, and distribute products to the customer?"

"Sure, without the customer, we don't have a business. But, that's not what we do in marketing. Our job is to be responsive to the customer needs, and work with the sales department to get things out the door."

"OK, so it's not a question of what must be done, but more of '… not marketing's job…' We're brainstorming today. Would you just accept the definition as part of the brainstorming, and let's talk about how we can make this a better business?"

"Sure. I'll go with whatever you like during the brainstorming."

"OK, Allie?" She nodded approval.

I'm going to break the marketing role into several activities, just so that we have some structure in the discussion." Jonathan launched a slide that included the topics:

    1.0   Definition of Marketing
    2.0   Brand

"I'm going to ask you to trust me about the definition of marketing as the core of our discussion today. At the end of the day, anything that you don't like about the definition, we'll change the definition. Agreed?"

All agreed.

Brand

"Let's talk about brand. Any thoughts?"

Nathan remained silent as Allie and Emily started the discussion.

Emily offered, "A brand is something intangible that tells people about a company."

"Do you mean a *brand* is a written statement that actually says, 'This Company sells inexpensive products,' or on the positive side, 'This Company sells 100% reliable products?'"

"No, I don't think a brand is written like that. More like people know what to expect. Maybe they say things like that elsewhere, but I don't think a brand is exactly a written statement."

"Allie, any thoughts?"

"I know a brand isn't tangible. I agree, I don't think it's a statement as much as what people expect, based on

89

everything a Company does every day. It is difficult for me to really explain it, but for example, when I think of Apple, I know if they sell a product, I know it's a good product."

"OK. I understand the Apple example. Good selection. But how do you know it's a good product."

Emily offered, "Because they are selling it. They have a great reputation."

"And do they ever say it's a great product?"

"Not at all. They don't have to. As a customer, I know it's a good product. They sell things that are easy to use."

"I like it, Emily. What else?"

"And they are easy to deal with."

"Explain please."

"Last year I bought a new iPhone from them. It should have been easy to use, to figure out all the features, but I'm not very technically oriented. I went to the Apple store, and one of their store Genius people sat down with me for 15 minutes showing me how to use the phone."

Emily added, "And the features in that phone are exactly what I needed, even though I didn't know I needed them."

"Interesting. How do you suppose that happened?"

"C'mon, Jonathan. You know as well as I do that Apple doesn't mess things up – like some other companies."

"So, does that mean that they design great products?"

"Better than great. They have some kind of intuition that helps them think like a user, then they design the functionality, make an elegant product that works every time."

"Interesting. We're talking about R&D, and manufacturing that help us believe in the Apple products."

"Anything else?"

"I trust them."

"And why?"

"I've seldom had a problem with any of their products, but two things… last year I bought a MacBook Pro from them. When I received the computer, it was clear that I needed more memory. I called the store, and they said, 'Bring it back for a full refund or exchange.' What the heck?

And two years ago, my 8-month old iPhone stopped working properly. I went to the store. They checked the original invoice and they gave me a new phone. Not only did they give me a new phone, they transferred all my data to the new phone – no charge."

While Emily and Allie were talking, Jonathan was writing on the white board.

BRAND

WHAT	WHO
intangible	engineering
expectations	r&d
daily	manufacturing
advertising	sales
relentlessly	customer service
good product	creative people
-design	grounds keepers
- features	maintenance
- manufacture	
- service	
instruction	
sales reps	
policies	
-sales	
-returns	
- warrantees	
trust	

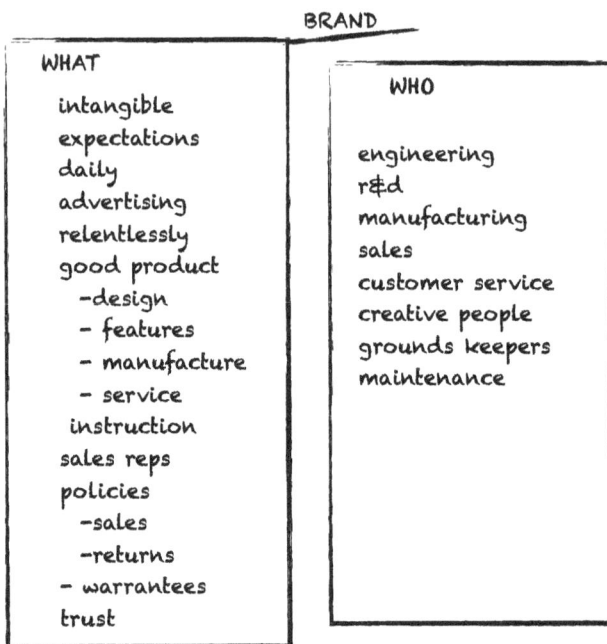

He stepped back from the board. "Anything I've missed?"

Allie, Emily, and Nathan scanned the whiteboard, thinking about their personal experiences with various companies.

Emily asked, "What we've described are things that apply to a great company that focuses on great service and high quality. Would a brand be any different for another kind of company?"

"Excellent question, Emily. Let's talk about Costco. What does their brand tell us?"

"Bulk."

"Inexpensive prices."

"Limited selection."

"Carefully curated product selection – likely higher quality than, let's say Walmart."

"Interesting that you bring up Walmart. How do their brands differ?"

"Walmart is definitely less expensive. They claim the lowest prices."

"Quality when compared to Costco?"

"Less quality. Generally, the employees try to be helpful, but they don't have the product knowledge that exists at Costco."

"Interesting that you discuss employees. Any thoughts?"

"I've heard that Costco provides higher pay, and better benefits than Walmart."

"So are the employees part of the brand image?"

"I never thought that employees could be part of brand, but as I think about it, it's part of the image that help establish expectations."

Jonathan was very pleased with the active discussion. "Excellent. So, let's summarize *BRAND* as we know it." He reviewed the whiteboard bullet points, and watched the body English of the marketing team.

Emily leaned forward, elbows on the conference table. "I'll be darned. When I came in this morning I knew that brand was a logo, and helped me make buying decisions, but I never understood the interaction among all the functions... the simple things that a company does that reinforce their brand position. I'll be darned."

Allie confirmed surprise. "I've never even thought about a definition of brand, and I'm still not sure that I understand the definition, but I have a much different impression."

"Who's in charge of brand?"

Nathan, silent until now, said, "I'll bite... marketing, right?"

"Yes, for sure that's the answer. But let's think about why. Marketing is analytical, responsible for understanding the Company's impact in the marketplace, how to get products launched, understand the company's marketing strategy. When I think of Finance, HR, Manufacturing, R&D – well, they have very specific functional responsibilities – finance & control, financial planning; manufacturing produces a product that fits the Company's strategy; R&D needs to develop new products that meet the Company's strategy. It looks like marketing needs to understand all those things to be effective."

Jonathan allowed a few minutes for the team to digest this summary. "So far today, we've talked about *marketing* and *brand*. Is there any reason we shouldn't continue?"

"Restroom break, Jonathan. Not just because you've put me on creative overload and I need a moment, but this Starbucks coffee has reached its limits. Can we break for 10 minutes?"

"Absolutely Emily. Back in 10 minutes."

Jonathan took the opportunity to huddle with Nathan. "Any thoughts, Nathan?"

"Only that I like the way you ask questions. You're not pontificating to us, but you're relying on us to draw conclusions. I can only guess that we're on the charted path that gets us to where we need to be."

"Right on, Nathan. Let's be clear. I don't know your business or your industry. I rely on your knowledge of both, and ask questions that take us down a path. This has been an excellent morning so far."

Just as Jonathan finished, Chuck walked in. "Mind if I join you?"

Competition

Nathan was first to respond. "Absolutely not... as long as Jonathan doesn't mind?"

"Ok with me. C'mon on in."

A few minutes later, Emily and Allie returned.

"Ladies, Chuck has decided to join us – great for us to get his knowledge in the process. Would anyone care to bring him up to speed in 2-3 minutes."

Emily volunteered, and provided an excellent summary of the early session.

Jonathan continued. "Excellent briefing, Emily. Now is actually perfect timing for Chuck to join us, as we begin to discuss *competition*.

I've taken a picture of the whiteboard, and we're starting with a sparkling clean sheet of *paper*." He wrote *COMPETITION* across the top.

"Just like this morning, talk to me about what we think the word competition means to Precision Technologies Inc."

"Competition – those are the companies that are trying to take our customers."

"Great. Would those only be current customers?"

"Not at all. That includes potential customers. But we also want their customers."

"I like the way you think, Nathan."

Jonathan continued to prod the team with questions – some simple – some more complex. After about 15 minutes, the pace of new information slowed. He stepped back to look at the board.

COMPETITION

customers
 - new customers
 - old customers
 - potential customers
other companies
new companies
domestic companies
international companies
new technology
products
product lines
geographic
indirect competitors
JV
high quality
low quality
low cost
better known

employees
agents
big companies
public companies
private companies
mom & pops

pricing
sales force
advertising

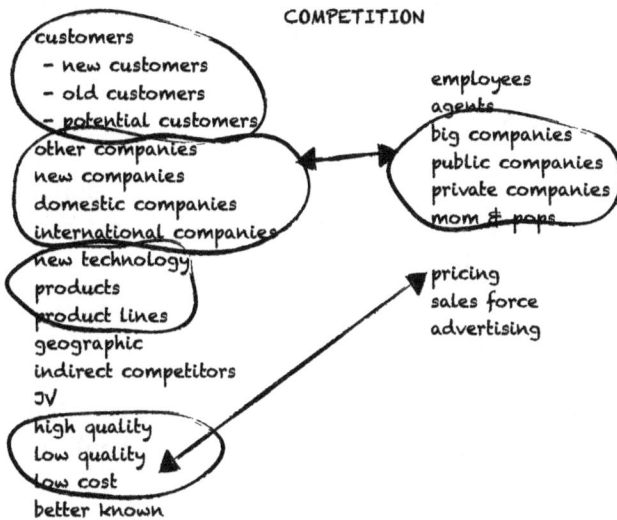

"We have quite a few points of information. When we think of competition, I've grouped into topical areas. Customers, companies, technology, and some branding things. Anything else we should talk about?"

After a minute of silence, Jonathan continued, "So what the heck should we do with this?"

Nathan suggested, "If we're going to retain customers and win new ones, I think we should know more about the competition."

"Any specifics?"

"In a perfect world, I'd like to know about their product pipeline… get a list of all their best customers… understand their market strategy…"

"That sounds like a great list, Nathan. Anyone else?"

Chuck now stood, "I'd like to know about their reps and how they are selling in the marketplace."

"Excellent. Others?"

"This may be totally off base, but if I knew how important the competitive product line was to them, would that help me better understand how they will compete?"

"Thanks, Emily. Can you explain?"

"If I'm a Fortune-500 Company with $10 billion of sales and our directly competitive products represented only $20 million of revenue, they may not be tough competitors."

"Keep going, Emily."

"Well, common sense says they'll prioritize to what matters most to them. If it's a mom & pop shop, and the product line represents 50% of their sales, they'll behave differently."

"Sort of survival mode?"

"Yes."

"Why does that matter?"

"They might discount more, or maybe spend more on advertising... more spending in the local community? I don't know, Jonathan, but if their livelihood depends on the product, I'd bet they might be tougher competitors."

"Got it. Great point Emily. Other thoughts? Let's say they have a faster new product development & launch process. Would that be an important factor?"

Nathan stood. "Exactly what we're facing now. We're getting beat up in the market by Textron. They've launched some new products with some specialty metals, and we're having a very tough time competing."

"Chuck, tell me about the sales force that we compete with. By the way, I'm very glad that you could join us."

"Competitor's sales force… funny that you mention that. The Textron gang is giving us a very difficult time. They've got the R&D to beat the hell out of us in new products, and their reps are traveling all over our territory with these white papers talking science while my guys are using last year's tech. It's like going to a gunfight without any bullets.

And I didn't mention that the mom & pops are killing me on price. These folks have been in the business for 25 years, make a great living, and aren't really aggressive with R&D, but heck, they're making a ton of money, so they're ok with a declining business."

"Would you call them bad competitors – meaning they are behaving irrationally in the market place."

"Good way to put it, Jonathan."

"What else out there?" After a few minutes, Jonathan stepped back and summarized. "We haven't hit all areas yet, but I see that when we talk about competition, we're talking various size companies, R&D resources, financial leverage, great sales forces etc. etc. etc. What do we do with that information?"

Chuck volunteered, "We make a game plan."

"Meaning just as in football, we try to win by concentrating on our strengths and weaknesses. We figure out how to win by minimizing our weaknesses, and using our strengths as the sharp point of the spear."

Nathan continued, "And we do that by understanding what our competitor's strengths & weaknesses are, and build a marketing strategy."

"I like it. Anyone else?"

Allie asked innocently, "Who does that?"

Chuck leaned back in his chair, smiled and said, "Let me guess… marketing?"

Jonathan replied, "Only if that makes sense, Chuck. Let's think out loud. To really understand the competition, we need many sources of information, we need to analyze, prioritize, and develop some kind of action plan. Chuck, your sales reps are in the field selling. Do they have the time to do the analysis?"

"Not if we're out in the field selling."

"And although R&D, manufacturing, logistics, finance and HR aren't in the room, will they have time to do the analysis and planning?"

"Not if they're doing their jobs."

Smiling, Jonathan summarized, "So I guess by default, Marketing gets the job. Comments?"

Chuck sighed, "Somehow you've taken me down this path before. I should've known that's where we'd end up. But let's be sure to understand that he can't just develop a marketing strategy by himself. He needs my team, R&D etc. Right?"

"Better than right … *right on!*"

Jonathan looked at Nathan. "Sounds like you'll need to do some kind of analysis. While we're thinking of it, let's just lay out a draft framework of some of the things that you could consider as you develop new products.

This is a first pass, and is by no means complete, but I think that we want to understand how big the market is… how much does it cost to develop the product… produce the product, and sell the product. Of course, every number is a best guess, but if we do the min-max approach, we've got the guardrails up to understand what we believe to be the major risks and opportunity."

"I like the min-max approach. What is the capex?"

"Some projects require unique manufacturing equipment. Just in case, I've added the line. This is just quick thinking to get you started."

```
                         NPD Analysis
                          Min       Probable      Max
Market Size (MIL $)
Units Sold
Avg Selling Price
Unit Cost
Development cost
Capex

Sales
Cost of sales
  Gross Profit

SG&A
```

Jonathan snapped a picture of the whiteboard, squirted the cleaning solution to have a clean sheet of *paper*.

He scanned the team and said, "What's next?"

Communications

Nathan said, "If we're following the agenda, it's communications."

"Right. When I talk about communications, what am I thinking? Allie?"

"What we tell the people outside the Company?"

"Excellent. Others"

The pattern continued with Jonathan plying the team with seemingly random questions, writing the responses on the white board.

After 15 minutes, he stepped back to review the brainstorming.

COMMUNICATION

inbound	outbound
surveys	rep script
customer feedback	collateral mat'l
FAQ's	advertising
reps	– print
trade associations	– radio
press	–tv
competitive websites	trade assoc
universities	– magazines
blogs	website
scientific papers	– written
bids lost	– audio
	– video
	– webinars
	white papers
	collaborative w univ
	community pr
	affiliations

"Now that is an outstanding list of communications. Any thoughts about how well we communicate?"

Silence.

After a few moments, Jonathan continued. "Look folks, unless you've focused on these issues, it's not unusual to miss some of these opportunities.

I think that if we reviewed each line item in this brainstorming list, we'd find that we have the talent and capability to deliver on any one of the items. It's just a matter of priority.

I'd like to take 10 minutes, and have you vote for the top 3 items that you think would provide the greatest benefit, with the most immediate impact."

Jonathan topped his coffee with some fresh brew as he waited for the vote. Each executive used the Post-its numbered 1-2-3 to select their top picks.

Jonathan summarized the top 3 picks for inbound and outbound communications, listed them on the board. "Let's develop an estimated time to complete each of these tasks."

The team discussed the amount of effort to complete each task, decided who would be responsible to complete the task, and when the effort should be done. Jonathan reminded them, "We're not after perfection with each of these tasks. Our goal is to have a quick impact on the market."

Top 3 Communications

Inbound	Who	Effort	When
1. Survey	1. Nathan	1. 40 hr	1. Q2
2. Rep input	2. Chuck	2. 2 hr/mo	2. Nxt Mo
3. Competitor Website	3. Nathan	3. 2 hr/mo	3. Not Mo

Outbound	Who		Who
1. Rep script	1. Nathan	1. 8 hr	1. Nxt Mo
2. Web blog	2. Chuck	2. 4 hr/mo	2. Nxt Mo
3. Collateral mat'l	3. Nathan	3. 40 hr	3. Q2

As he stepped back to look at the board, he complimented the team.

"Now let's consider what we've just done. We know that we have limited resources, but we've identified tasks that would be beneficial to the Company, estimated the amount of effort required to complete the task, and assigned an executive sponsor who will ensure the task will be completed. Except for the survey, we haven't spent any money. And if we like, we can complete a limited survey using Survey Monkey at no cost.

Ladies and gentleman – congratulations on this effort. This is the first cut at communications, but there may be other tasks to add later."

All nodded agreement.

Product

"You folks are making this easy for me. I can't remember the last time I've had such a creative group. Now let's shift to product. Let me ask a few questions to light up the topic.

First of all, when was the last time we pruned the product line?"

Nathan was quick to respond. "We haven't done that since I've been here. We want to be sure we don't lose any customers by not having what they're accustomed to ordering."

"Do we know what our old outdated product portfolio looks like? How much inventory we have... what is its

105

value? How much space is dedicated to the outdated inventory?"

Brad responded, "I don't think that we've ever identified those items."

"So, I guess that we don't know if that old inventory on the books costs me $1,000 or $100,000 of carrying cost, space, insurance, handling etc. True?"

"I guess that's true," Nathan responded.

"Do we know if any of that old inventory ever gets reordered? For example, have we put a hold on replenishing the stocks?"

"I'm not sure."

"And if we were to mistakenly reorder, is there a minimum order size required that will build our old inventory?"

"… not sure."

"And are we comfortable with those answers?"

Brad leaned forward, elbows on the table. "I think we should at least know some of the basics before we just assume the topic of outdated products away. Ben, I think that the research should be yours. Agreed?"

It was clear that Ben did not want the work to do but had to accept the responsibility. Jonathan summarized the next steps on a slide.

Old/obsolete inventory

−define obsolete	Ben	Q2
−take physical inventory	Ben	Q2
−reconcile to book	Marissa	Q2
−summarize carrying cost	Marissa	Q2
−policy recommendations	Ben/Marissa/Nathan/Chuck	Q2

"Let's move on to new product pipeline. What's our new product pipeline look like?"

"Pipeline might be a bit of an overstatement, Jonathan."

"And why do you say that Emily?"

"Well we really don't have what might be considered a pipeline... a flow of new products. We've relied on the reps to identify the needs based on customer and market observation, and when they bring in a new product idea, we evaluate whether it makes sense."

"Is that a formal process. For example, is there a quarterly meeting to discuss the market trends?"

"More ad hoc than a systematic process."

"Got it. Is there a formalized process to evaluate the value of a potential new product? For example, if a rep brings in a concept, do Nathan and Chuck sit with R&D and Manufacturing to discuss sales and profit potential? Maybe even include the CFO?"

"There's no formal review process, Jonathan."

"How important is new product development in the industry?"

Nathan, with a concerned look, commented. "It's quite important since we're in a highly competitive industry. Not only is design critical, but new materials can potentially flip the market on its ear. I'd say it is very important."

"Comments."

Chuck immediately responded. "Without new products and a promise of new products, my reps are at a disadvantage. It would be great to have a reason to visit my best customers with news about new products, or new technology."

"Is it fair to say we'd like new product development to be a priority?"

"Fair enough, but it's something that maybe we can't afford."

"How does playing catch up fit with our brand strategy of '1st class'?"

After a few moments of deadly silence, Jonathan continued, "Is it fair to say that playing catch-up is not consistent with a brand strategy of 1st class?"

In a quiet voice, Nathan, while staring at the conference table, responded. "Yes - inconsistent."

"OK. Let's not beat each other up. Does this mean that we have a wonderful upside?"

Jonathan paused.

"Let me phrase it another way. We've done just fine for the past few years without a new product pipeline process… being followers in the market. We've identified an opportunity to potentially lead the market. What will happen to earnings if we do that?"

In a more positive voice – a voice with energy, Nathan smiled and said, "Now that really is an opportunity."

Chuck added, "Remember that Santa wish list from a few days ago? Well, there you go. Nothing but upside, Jonathan."

Jonathan added several notes to the whiteboard … added some arrows and highlight boxes. "Anybody want to comment?"

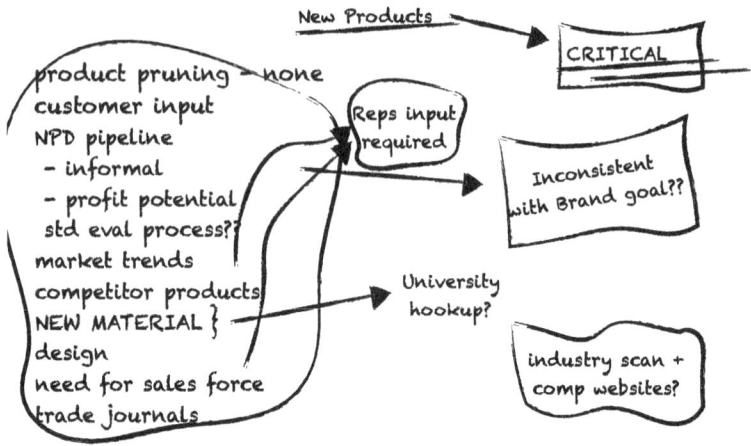

New Products → CRITICAL

product pruning — none
customer input
NPD pipeline
  - informal
  - profit potential
std eval process??
market trends
competitor products
NEW MATERIAL }
design
need for sales force
trade journals

Reps input required

Inconsistent with Brand goal??

University hookup?

industry scan + comp websites?

Allie looked somewhat puzzled. "Do I see some of the same things on this new product page as I saw in communications, and brand?"

"You betcha, Allie. Thoughts?"

"I'm guessing that you want us to conclude that there is an overlap among the things that make up marketing."

"That'll do just fine, Chuck. Any other comments?"

"How should we evaluate potential new products?"

"Great question, Nathan. Let's spend a few minutes and sketch important things in any new product development process." For the next 10 minutes they discussed the NPD process, important criteria to evaluate new products, and agreed on a rough format.

"How does that look for a starter? It's more detailed than our earlier list from this week."

Emily observed, "Looks like a lot of work."

"Yes, Emily, but by thinking through NPD in a systematic way, we won't waste money on things that just don't make sense. If we don't think through these issues BEFORE we start spending money, what's the result?"

Brad interrupted. "I like the concept Jonathan. I'm not sure that it's a final form, but I'd like to start using that format right away. Let's keep going. This is great stuff."

R&D Analysis	Min	Probable	Max
Market Size (MIL $)			
Units Sold			
Avg Selling Price			
Unit Cost			
Lab			
Mat'l			
O/H			
Other			
Total Cost			
000's $			
Development cost			
– R&D Time			
– R&D Mat'l			
– Outsourced			
– Overhead			
Total Cost			
Capex			
Sales			
Cost of sales			
Gross Profit			
SG&A			
Direct Selling			
Advertising			
Promotional mat'l			
Samples			
Video's			
Other cost			
Total Cost			
Pretax Profit			

Nathan smiled. "You're making us go through a lot of work to take us where you want to go. … garden path Jonathan."

"On the one hand I agree with you, but when you look at where we started, I'm only using your inputs to guide this conversation."

"Yeah… yeah… I get it, Jonathan. I agree with everything that we've written and concluded, Mr. Columbo."

Chuck and Nathan laughed out loud. Emily and Allie looked at each other with a blank stare.

Marketing Mix

Jonathan continued. "Enough about product. Let's jump into marketing mix. Let's start with a definition – our own terms, team. Thoughts?"

By now the team was accustomed to his mode of operation.

Chuck immediately said, "Everything that we do to help sell product."

"Excellent, Chuck. What does sell product mean?"

"Get in front of the customer to get the order."

"Right. So, it's a sales function. Anything else."

Emily leaned forward, "I'm going to guess that since we spent a lot of time discussing brand, it would include the brand things."

"Which are?"

"Well, communications, new product development, um…"

"Compensation… commission plans, advertising, website, community relations…"

"Ok – now we're rolling. Keep shouting things out, while I jot some notes. Make me work folks."

Sales **Stuff**	**Marketing Mix Funds Avail**	**What if**
- salary		
- commission	$14 M	$18 M
- SPIFS		
- T		
- &E		
advertising		
- print	$4 M	$1 M
- TV		
- Google/click	$2 M	$4 M
Brochures & collateral		
Website		
- words	$3 M	$1 M
- video		
- blogs		
Marketing Comp		
Surveys		
Trade shows	$3 M	$3 M
Public relations		
- university $	$3 M	$3 M
Trade Assoc		$0 M
Donations	$1 M	
Community relations	$30 M	$30 M

After a few more minutes of brainstorming the list included about 20 categories.

"I'm going to be arbitrary and just make up some numbers to push the envelope. We now see how Precision Technologies will spend its money in the first column of values. Reasonable or just plain silly?"

"It's certainly not accurate, but it's not plain stupid."

"And when I do a 'what if', and spend a lot more money in the sales operations - good or bad?"

Chuck smiled. "I like the what if?"

"Other thoughts?"

"I'm not sure that cutting the advertising and reducing community support is a good idea."

"Why is that Nathan?"

"Part of our overall image is that of a quality Company. One that takes care of its own, and we're a part of the community."

"Should we add back the $1 million? Where would you like the advertising to be?"

"I don't know the exact number, but we have several programs that we know add to the Company brand."

"Let's list some of them."

Nathan listed several advertising and community expenditures that all agreed would impact the brand if we discontinued spending.

"Where shall we get the money from? We've got a $30-million-dollar limit."

"There only one major category, other than cutting my salary. I think we need to reduce the Sales expense."

"Chuck - your thoughts?"

"You're not making this very easy, Jonathan. I know that the programs Nathan listed are key to our quality image. I hate to give up sales money, but I understand.

Wait a minute, why are we limited to $30 million?"

"Because that's the limit, given 4% increase in sales."

"Who says we'll only grow by 4%?"

"Now that is an excellent question, Chuck. Thoughts?"

"Earlier we discussed the competitive environment. We've got an opportunity to grow this business, and if we capture that opportunity, we may have more money to invest. Didn't we say that we had a small market share?"

"On the grand scale, we've got room to grow. But to make that happen, we'll need some new products."

"How will we get new products?"

"R&D. But that's not within the marketing mix discussion that we're working on."

"Right. But if our strategy includes new products – by working with universities… listening to the sales reps feedback… watching the websites of competitors and participating in the trade associations, we may be able to accelerate the NPD process."

"I agree with all that. But right now, we're concentrating on the Marketing Mix. What if we just start with the funds available as of today, and decide what actions we can take to improve the business. For example, a minute ago I heard that competitive intelligence was important. What if we set up some standard Google search macros for our competitors, Nathan? Good or bad?"

"That can't take too much time. And if I understand how that works, we get daily notifications when a competitor shows up in the news."

"That's right. And if we were interested in certain technologies, could we also set up search macros for that?"

"Absolutely."

"We also mentioned surveys. Do we have any feedback loops in our website? Customer comments? Or frequently asked questions?"

"We've got the FAQ's, but we don't look at the site very often."

"Missed opportunity?"

"Only if that source of information is more important than what Emily and Allie are doing today."

"Ladies, do you think you can prioritize these activities into your monthly routine without adversely affecting your deliverables?"

"Absolutely."

Jonathan continued the 'what-if' routine for the next half-hour, listing specific activities that could be completed today, without any increased spending. As the team identified actions, they seemed to be more excited about the business. Jonathan has seen this same phenomenon at every brainstorming session. The key is to get the team focused on what could be done, rather than identify reasons why something couldn't be done.

ZERO cost Actions
- company search
- people search
- white papers (r&d)
- Marketing speaking
- update brochures

After recording the suggestions of no/low cost actions, Jonathan suggested, "We're not going to be able to sort out the final marketing mix in today's meeting. Is it fair to say that we have a different idea about how to challenge our internal priorities and think differently about how we approach the market?"

All agreed.

Jonathan also noted, "We've gotten so tied up in the daily activity – I'll call it getting sucked into a work vortex – that we haven't been able to challenge some of the activities. Not that they were a waste of time – but there may be a better way to use the resource. I think that we've got to sit down with Brad, Joanne and Marissa to make the hard calls on how we spend the money."

"I think it's clear that it's a team effort with many places to spend the limited amount of money available. Who said 'sales might increase?'"

Chuck smiled, "That would be me, Jonathan. We've never thought so radically as you've suggested, but it seems that growth is possible if we focus our resources. Just like in football, you design the plays to get greatest advantage against the opposition. We'll have to develop some plays."

"Folks, this has been a great day. When I look at all the analysis that we've completed, I can only say, congratulations. Great effort on your part. I especially liked the way we focused on the Company objective of beating the competition. Chuck, I think that we're on for tomorrow. You know the plan and how I work. Who will be attending?"

"I'll have my best reps here for the discussion. Nathan, interested in joining us? It may be helpful as part of your understanding of the sales part of the marketing mix."

"I'm booked until 10AM, but I'll join you around then if that makes sense."

"Makes sense to me." The meeting adjourned.

Chuck & Sales Staff Meet with Jonathan
Sales

This morning the conference room was nearly filled. Chuck and Nathan were there, as well as 4 of Chuck's sales reps. When Jonathan arrived, he was a surprised by the number of people, but he'd always found that the more participants – up to about 10 – the better. This gave him a cross-section of the true environment.

"Welcome Chuck, Nathan. Nathan, glad you could start the day with us… a pleasant surprise. Thanks for joining us. And Chuck, it looks like you've brought some reinforcements. That's great. I like working with field reps as well as the executive team.

Let's begin the process." He explained his methods to the reps who were not in attendance yesterday.

Jonathan invited each rep to give a brief bio before the formal meeting started. One rep, Jack, was a worrisome participant. Employed at Precision for about 13 years, he seemed like he had a chip on his shoulder. His introduction played like a Marvel Superhero bio… yes, definitely he'd be a challenge.

"Let's talk about the sales function. Any thoughts about sales."

Jack immediately responded, "Get the orders… without us, the Company's got problems."

"Excellent – 'Get sales', as he scrawled it across the board. "And how do we do that? Do we just arrive at an office and ask for the order?"

Once again, Jack volunteered, "It's one hell of a lot more than that, Jonathan. We spend hours researching the customer, always trying to find that advantage that we have compared to our competitors. And then we compare our product lines to their requirements. If we're really good, we'll get a large order that will keep our competitors out for a few months."

"Large orders. Excellent. Anything else?"

Bill, the youngest sales rep, raised his hand, awaiting acknowledgement. "Yes, Bill."

"I like to spend time with the customer … listen to them talk about their business. Usually I don't get any more than 30 minutes face time, but I want to hear about their business, not just sell them out of our catalog."

"That's curious. Why wouldn't you just sell the catalog."

"I'm fairly new with Precision, and it isn't as easy for me to understand their requirements as quickly as the more experienced folks like Jack. I try to listen to what they are doing in their business, and as a rookie I get to ask questions that might seem naive.

That helps me identify a better potential solution for their business. Sometimes, as we're talking about what they're doing, I've had the chance to suggest some additional products that they hadn't considered before."

"Like what?"

"We have some unique technical skills in certain metallurgical fields. I'm a curious person, and when I have the chance, I talk with our engineering guys to understand what they're working on. It has to be a pain in the butt for them since I ask for layman's terms, not the PhD level scientific terminology, but when *I* understand it, *I* can explain it to others.

I can share some of those technical features with the client's purchasing agent. I guess that the purchasing agent and I are often at the non-technical level of engineering."

As Jonathan continued to encourage Jack, he scratched 'listening' on the board.

Sales process

Get orders
customer research
compare prod lines to competition
large orders
Understand customer needs
listen to customer
suggest new products
metallurgy unique
reps spend time with engineers
engineering info in layman's terms
windshield time
review shipments
expedite orders
get price change approvals
current customers
potential customers

"That's quite a list of sales activities. Excellent start. … moving on.

We visit the customer and try to get an order. What clients do we call on? Any priorities?"

"I group my clients into geography so that I reduce my windshield time."

"Great Claire. Anything else?"

"Whenever I can, I visit potential customers."

"And how do you identify potentials? Do you just visit companies in the area that aren't customers?"

"I try to visit potentials, but for sure I'll try to get an appointment with the major potential companies as a priority?"

"What's a major?"

A-B-C Customer Classification

"Just one that I think is a large potential account."

"Have we defined A-B-C classifications?"

Bill asked, "What's A-B-C classification?"

"It's a somewhat arbitrary classification of what are the most important customers – actual or potential – based on annual sales volume. Companies will run a high-low listing of their customers last year's sales, and pick a revenue number – for here an 'A' account might be annual revenue greater than $500k; a 'C' account might have annual revenue of $25k. Everything between $25k-$500k is a 'B' account.

Companies use these reference points to establish priorities. Would you rather have two $500k accounts or two accounts with less than $25k?"

Bill quickly responded, "I'll take the 'A' accounts any day."

"Great, then you get the idea. It gets even more analytical when we slice & dice yet again. We'd like to separate the 'A' actual and 'A' potential accounts. Any guess why?"

Claire offered, "Because they may need a different sales method?"

Bill added, "And different sales resources?"

"Both correct. Let's talk about a cold call on a potential 'A' account versus a call on an established 'A' account. Is there any process difference?"

Jack jumped in. "Of course there is. For an established 'A' account, we already have a working relationship. They know who we are, generally our complete product line, so there is a lot less education of an existing account.

We also have different expectations. When I call on an 'A' account, I'd like to walk away with an order almost every time. With a potential account, it's unlikely that I get an order when I call on them for the first time. I may have to call on them several times before I get an order."

"Do you call on them with any established frequency?

"For an 'A' prospect, it probably takes 9-12 months to eventually get an order."

"Let's say you make a first call. What would you normally do?"

"I'd have our Company annual report – that would be an abbreviated report not showing confidential information, but something that talks about our approximate size, product lines, maybe some reference customers."

"Expectations?"

"While I'd like to get an order, I'd really be happy to visit for 30 minutes."

"And then?"

"Depending on the time of year, I might invite them to our trade show booth? I'd certainly get them on my private mailing list so that I could have a personal follow-up in a few weeks. I'd also be sure that they receive a personal note about any new product launches we have."

"Do you get many new products?"

"Not enough."

"Anything else?"

"If I spot any news about their business, I'd drop them a note, but other than that, it would be a follow-up call every few months. I'd do that for maybe 6 months, then I'd put them on an unusual event cycle."

"Claire and Bill, any comments?"

Claire first spoke. "I've got something like that, but I don't have any structured call cycle. And I haven't identified any end point for when I stop calling on them."

"Bill?"

"I've been trying to standardize the best way to call on potential customers… maybe even standardize regular customers, but I'm not there yet."

"Would it be worthwhile to develop a standard process that could be used throughout the Company as a guide? Not too rigid, but it seems that Jack has a tremendous amount of experience that could be mined for his wisdom?"

Bill and Claire both agreed.

Jonathan continued to press for ways that the Company could do better to improve the sales experience. Once he had a list of about 25 ideas, he asked the participants to rank the top 5 needs.

Actions

Actions
- google company search
- google people search
5 - white papers (r&d)
- marketing speeches
4 - update brochures
4 - newsletter
1 - new product launches
3 - standard pipeline stages
- standard call cycles
2 - CRM
- master reporting
3 - improved financial reporting
- testimonials

Actions
4 2 - in house call center
2 - on-line ordering
- on-line shop manuals
- expanded FAQ's on website
- website videos
- Webinars
5 - sales training
3 - product training
- more reps

Jonathan stepped back from the board, looked at the top 5 needs, and asked, "As a group, if we were to be able to complete the ideas circled, would that be the best way to improve sales operations here at the Company?"

The sales reps and Chuck discussed the encircled items for about 10 minutes.

Chuck summarized. "I think that if we did the following, we'd have a better sales results here at the Company:
- More new products
- Standard pipeline stages

- In-house call center
- On-line ordering
- Updated brochures
- A CRM system to manage the accounts
- Product training

Jonathan smiled broadly. "Excellent. We not only have identified many opportunities for improving sales at Precision Technologies Inc., we've prioritized the activities, based on your input. What's next?"

Sales Coverage

Jonathan continued. "When I think of a sales force and hundreds of customers… perhaps hundreds of potential customers, how do we approach selling to such a broad group?"

"Chuck leaned forward. "We let the reps determine how they manage their territories."

"OK, reps, talk to me."

Bill politely raised his hand. "I like to call on my biggest customers at least monthly. While I may not have anything new for them, I want to keep the Company name above the radar."

"Great. And other than your largest customers?"

"I guess the next tier – the 'B's' - I like to talk with them at least quarterly."

"Got it. And how about potential customers? Do you have a master list that you routinely contact?"

"Well, yes, but I don't really have a systematic requirement to reach out to them. My goal, I guess, is that I should talk with them at least twice a year."

"Interesting. The goal is twice a year. How successful are you with that?"

"That's something that I haven't really tracked. I have a definite focus on the current customers... the largest, and maybe the second tier."

"Good or bad?"

Bill felt awkward with the questions. In a lowered voice, "I guess it's not the brightest thing – you know, not calling more frequently on the major potential customers."

"Not a big deal, Bill. We're exploring. I'll respond with - you're keeping the current 'A' customers very happy, right?"

"Yes, but it seems like a missed opportunity."

Sales Rep Time Analysis

"Could be, but let's focus on what can be rather than what has been. Going back to an earlier discussion. An all-in sales call – research, prep, travel, follow-up for a 30 minutes sales call could take up to 3-4 hours. When we look at a quarter – let's call it 13 weeks at 40 hours/week, that's 520 hours. Could we set an arbitrary goal of 8 "A" potential sales calls a quarter, and measure against that goal?"

"Seems reasonable. It sure doesn't sound overpowering to me."

"Now let's dive into the lower levels of customers. Let's say we define 'B' customers with annual volume of $25k - $500k. How often have you touched them?"

"Unfortunately, I don't have any record."

"And another question. Is it possible that a 'B' customer could be an 'A' customer – we just haven't penetrated the account sufficiently?"

"That's definitely possible."

"So, maybe we shouldn't be concentrating only on 'A' *actual* customers?"

"Seems like a reasonable choice to spend more time on 'A' potentials who are already customers."

"Going back to the call rates per quarter – how many of the 'A' potential, 'B' accounts do we call on every quarter?"

"… couldn't tell you."

"Not a problem. And how do we sell to the 'C' customers?"

"I can't afford the time to visit the 'C' customers, unless they are filler appointment during the 'A & B' trips."

"So how do we sell to them?"

Chuck was getting irritated with this cross-examination of one of his reps. "Let's back off the questions, Jonathan.

Bill does a helluva job. He operates just like the rest of us."

"I understand, Chuck. I don't mean to focus on Bill. In general, do any of the reps do anything significantly different?"

Silence.

"OK, rather than focus on how we operate today, let's just pretend we have an open slate. We have actual and potential A-B-C accounts. I think that we'd all agree that to send a rep to every customer would be prohibitively expensive. "

All nodded agreement.

"And that we have limited resources. What do you think we should do to sell to all classes of customers?"

For the next 15 minutes, the sales team brainstormed about the types of sales *contacts or touches* the Company could have. Jonathan quickly listed them on the board.

(000's $)	A		B		C		Total		
	Act	Pot	Act	Pot	Act	Pot	Act	Pot	Total
Sales Rep									
Salary									
Commiss									
T&E									
SPIF									
Reps									
Call center									
Brochures									
Website									
Trade Shows									
New Prod Launch									
Other									
Total	35	10	30	10	10	5	75	25	100

"I'll admit, I've made up some numbers. When we look at the allocation that I've scratched out, what do you think?"

Chuck stared intently at the matrix. "If I understand this correctly, you're saying that we should allocate 45% of our total selling effort to the 'A' actual and potential customers. And also, that we should spend 10% of our entire sales resource on 'A' potential customers?"

"Chuck, I'm not smart enough to tell you that. What I've done is create a straw-man as an example. It's up to you and your team to think through the sales process.

A question. 'Would a website designed exclusively for the 'A' class customer be different from that designed for a 'C' class customer?"

Bill and Chuck looked at each other. Chuck offered, "I guess they might. But I can't tell you exactly what might be different."

"I think at this time, we just want to determine that things could be a different design. The elements of the design will be for a later time.

How about brochure design? Any differences?"

Allie responded, "Sure there would be differences. We might want more technical information for the more sophisticated Fortune 500 company. We might want some videos for the 'B' and 'C' accounts."

Jonathan looked up from his notes, "Videos?"

"Sure. I've seen some very nice videos on industrial sites. They've even had some – what are they called – testimonials? But some sites just have an introduction of the owners, maybe a factory tour, and introduction of some of the key employees. Makes it more personal for the customers.

I've seen some with on-line ordering… maybe even service manuals on the site so the customer has everything they need to perform at their best."

"Wow, Allie. Comments anyone?"

Bill added, "I've seen recruiting on the sites. And some include highlights of their community support activities. Just last week, Johnson Limited had a video of some of their employees working on the 'Habitat for Humanity' project in Cincinnati."

Playing the Devil's Advocate, Jonathan said, "What the heck does that have to do with selling to customers? Seems like a waste of time & money to me."

Nathan tapped his pen on the table, as if to ask for permission to speak. "I'll tag that as a company culture thing. I can guess that kind of company spirit could be very appealing to some potential employees."

"Ahah. The website can be used for recruiting as well as selling product."

Nathan said, "Let's call it reinforcing our brand, Jonathan. Outbound communication."

They were starting to embrace the brand image, and link several functional areas to the Company image. "You've got me, Nathan. I agree 100%. Thoughts?"

Chuck leaned back in his chair. "OK Jonathan. I'm picking up a pattern here. Do I see that *BRAND* is all encompassing? Employees, customers etc.?"

"Only if it makes sense in your business…"

Chuck smiled…

Spending Model - Analysis

After scanning the list of all possible ways to sell to the 'A-B-C' potential customers, Jonathan summarized. "That's more of a wish list. I'm not sure that we can afford to do those things circled. I think that we've got to talk with Marissa and IT to find out how much these will cost and how long it will take to implement. Then we'll have to talk with Brad to see if we can get the money."

Actions

Actions
- google company search
- google people search
- 5 –white papers (r&d)
- marketing speeches
- 4 –update brochures
- 4 –newsletter
- 1 –new product launches
- 5 –standard pipeline stages
- standard call cycles
- 2 –CRM
- master reporting
- 3 –improved financial reporting
- testimonials
-

Actions
- 4 2 –in house call center
- 2 –on-line ordering
- on-line shop manuals
- expanded FAQ's on website
- website videos
- Webinars
- 5 –sales training
- 3 –product training
- more reps
-

"What will Marissa be asking for?"

Bill volunteered, "Probably how much will the program cost, and what and when can we expect a financial return."

"Fair enough." Jonathan continued. "How will you estimate the value of each of those items?"

"Educated guess. But we won't be very educated… more guess than anything else."

"We'll be evaluating risk?"

All agreed.

"May I suggest that we use the min-max-probability model?"

Jonathan went to the whiteboard and started writing, while talking them through the model.

"Let's play with a *Call Center* model. This kind of modelling will always be best guess, but who better than you folks to estimate. Let's look at the basic elements. We've got the Min-Probable-Max, and the labels relate to the dollar impact and the estimated likelihood of success.

Our goal with the analysis is to think through each activity that we need to make the project work. So, for example, you'll see that we have a capital cost. Any idea what's in there?"

"Most likely the cost of the call center equipment and software... maybe the renovations we'd make to the office."

"That's right Claire."

"I don't understand why development costs have such a broad range."

Call Center		1st Year	
	Min	Probable	Max
Probability	30%	50%	20%
(000's $)			
Sales	400	550	1000
Gross Profit	200	275	500
SG&A			
Developmei	25	40	80
Salary	45	45	80
Training	5	5	5
All Other			
Total SG	75	90	165
Pretax Cont	125	185	335
Capital	20	35	60

"That is what sometimes happens with software development. Costs go through the roof."

"How will we get the costs?"

"Your IT person may be able to get some very good estimates, but for sure there are many consultants that have installed call center software. I don't want to get too deep into this particular model, but basically, you're going to simulate what you expect to happen when you launch the process.

Probabilities are best guess, and that's a condition of the analysis. We're trying to predict the future, which always has risk.

One other thing. You'll notice that I used nearest thousand dollars. Predicting the future isn't exact. Don't get hung up on a few hundred dollars +-. There is that much error in any estimate that you prepare. For example, if a call center part-timer who works 1,000 hours, and gets paid $15/hour, but could get as much as $17/hour, how much impact will that have on the analysis? There is more than a 10% error in your estimate, so don't agonize over a few dollars. It's not accounting, but forecasting.

"We've identified 6 priorities. Nathan, Chuck – can I list you as co-sponsors to do a min-max with Marissa in the next quarter?"

Both agreed.

Typical Sales Call

Jonathan continued, "When I think of sales, I think of time as a critical resource. Have you thought about where you spend your time every day or week?"

Bill responded. "I try to keep track of my time to always be doing something positive. During the past 6 months, I've probably spent about 75% of my time in front of customers… 10% of my time with the engineers getting educated, and about 15% of my time on reports. And the 75% includes travel time."

"Thanks Bill. Any others?"

Jack perked up during the discussion. "I'm totally focused on the customer. I spend all my time with customers – either on the phone, in the car or in their office. Sometimes, I also take them out for a golf or tennis match."

"And Claire? Any thoughts?"

"I'm fairly new, like Bill, and it seems that I spend a lot of time trying to figure out what we've sold to some of my customers. I spend time looking at computer reports trying to find out if I've made any commission. But I don't spend time keeping track of my time like Bill. I think maybe I should – but that might take time away from the selling."

Jonathan continued to push. "Do you have enough new *stuff* to make a visit worthwhile?"

Chuck asked, "What is *stuff*? Do you mean new products? No, never enough. What else are you talking about?"

"How about a reason to be there. New technology or a research discussion? Maybe some trends that you've identified in the industry. New materials that will help the client better understand how we can help them? Jack, you mentioned that you do research. What does that include?"

"Good question. I check the A/R to find out if customers have any old balances, check my personal files so that I understand any correspondence since the last meeting … check out the competition to hear what they've got going. Just in general, I want a lot of information before I go to an 'A or B' client."

"Sounds like good preparation. Claire, Bill? What kind of research do you do?"

"Pretty much the same thing. Jack, I didn't realize that you checked out the competition. Can you share the info with us?"

"Sure Bill. And for you too Claire."

Jonathan interrupted. "I'm guessing that you google key words, right?"

"Yes."

"Have you considered having the marketing department develop some macros for all our competitors so that we don't do the research 3 times – once for Jack, Bill and Claire?"

"Jonathan, marketing doesn't have the time to do that."

Jonathan circled competitor research and continued. "As a sales team, do we ever establish national targets and coordinate our efforts? For example, Textron probably has locations in virtually every territory..."

"National targets? We haven't so far. Each Textron division is autonomous."

"If we do a great job with one of their divisions, do you think it would be worthwhile to ask for a referral to other divisions? I can't imagine a more qualified or credible referral than a sister division?"

Attendees were silent for a moment.

"Does anyone use LinkedIn during their research? I've heard some great success stories about a fraternity brother referral that turned into great business?"

Jack scowled, "Web nonsense... not very helpful in our business, so I don't use it."

Claire politely raised her hand. "I've used LinkedIn for data mining. The software provides insight into a person or company's network. The information for a few of those cold calls that I've made has been very helpful. I now know why people have often said, 'be careful what you put on the web.' It's shocking what I've found when researching some corporate executives."

"Cold calls … How much of our time do we spend prospecting?"

The prospecting time commitment varied among the sales reps. Jack spent little time prospecting, since he had a well-established set of customers.

Claire and Bill dedicated – their estimate – about 5% of their time prospecting.

"Do we think that 5% is enough?"

After a brief pause, "Let's continue."

Customer Portfolio - Turnover

"What is our customer turnover rate?"

"On average, we lose about 5-10% of our customers each year?"

"Do we know why they leave us? Any trends in the data?"

Chuck responded, "Sometimes they sell the business and the new owners have established relationships with competitors. Sometimes the customer dies and the linkage goes with them, or maybe our pricing is too high. There are many reasons, Jonathan."

"What are the trends?"

Chuck seemed embarrassed. "Maybe we should spend more time analyzing trends. But I don't think we have a major problem."

"If I were to guess, the top 3 categories were service, pricing, and product selection, would I be far off?"

"Probably not. Of the customers I've lost, those are the top reasons."

"Have we lost any major accounts recently?"

"If you mean 'A' accounts, no, but we've lost several 'B' accounts in the last 6 months."

"Why have they left us?"

"I think it was a combination of two things… technology, and pricing. We didn't do any serious kind of debriefing – they didn't want to spend the time with us. But during the past year, they have mentioned several times that our technology needed to improve. They also mentioned that our pricing relative to our technology was out of line."

"Didn't they also have some problems with our service? As I recall, they had several time-sensitive orders that we weren't able to deliver on schedule."

"That may have had some impact."

Jonathan followed up, "When we lose a customer – maybe not every customer but the A's and B's – do we debrief the customer? Could this be a great source of research? Or better yet, when the reps hear of customer concerns, do we have a systematic way of summarizing the information?"

Chuck responded, "We don't have a formal way of summarizing customer feedback. Maybe we should include that in our monthly sales meetings?"

"Works for me," Bill offered.

Jonathan continued his probing questions for the next 30 minutes, all the while jotting notes on the whiteboard. Jack was continuously dominating the discussion, while Claire and Bill contributed when they thought they had helpful information.

Sales Resource

Sales Rep
  Salary
  Commiss
  T&E
  SPIF
Reps
Call center
Brochures
Website
Trade Shows
New Prod Launch
Other
  Total

After 30 minutes, Jonathan turned to the whiteboard with many notes – some circled indicating a priority.

"Let's think about how we allocate our resources among A-B-C actual and potential clients. Chuck, we've seen this before, but let's engage the sales force. Again, this is not an accounting exercise.

When I think of your responsibility to cover the A-B-C's and actual and potential, you're going to have to determine how much resource you dedicate to each segment. So, in this example, 'A' accounts get about 45% of all your resources.

That indicates that you expect your best returns to come from accounts with more than – did we say $500k of annual sales. This matrix shows that you want to invest 45% of your resources to protect and/or recruit your 'A' actual and potential customers.

'C' accounts only receive about 15% of your resources. But that 15% of resources probably get most of the call center costs, and very little of the rep salary costs.

When you look at the totals for each segment, that will be your judgment about the importance of the segment. This isn't an exact science, but rather intuition. It's not exact accounting, but an analysis that uses judgment to measure relative importance of investing resources. Let's poke at the matrix a bit.

We all know that you can't decide exactly how much benefit a brochure is to an 'A-B-C' customer. Or how much value the website is to a 'C' customer.

But I think that we'd all agree that somehow we'd like to touch all the customers in some way during the course of a year. By designing some elements of the sales mix, we can directly affect the results. When we look at the matrix, we might also find that a greater amount of the commissions will be dedicated to the Potential 'A and B' accounts that will give you long term growth. Higher salaries may be allocated to the existing accounts. I know this sounds a bit complicated, but when you're dealing with round numbers, you'll be thinking about solving the problem of allocating the resources rather than balancing the spreadsheet to the nearest dollar. Questions?"

Chuck stood and studied the matrix. "So how long do you think this kind of analysis should take?"

"Just to give it some shape, maybe a half-day, since we're concentrating on the thought process rather than exact dollar amounts."

(000's $)	A		B		C		Total		
	Act	Pot	Act	Pot	Act	Pot	Act	Pot	Total
Sales Rep									
Salary									
Commiss									
T&E									
SPIF									
Reps									
Call center									
Brochures									
Website									
Trade Shows									
New Prod Launch									
Other									
Total	35	10	30	10	10	5	75	25	100

CRM

"Can we spend a few minutes on the CRM reporting that surfaced in the top ten categories? Who wants to drive on this?"

Claire volunteered. "Right now, I use an Excel spreadsheet to manage my accounts, and it's a pain. I don't have enough information in the spreadsheet to really understand what's happening. I now manage about 120 accounts – many of them 'C' accounts. But the 'A & B' level accounts are very important to me. I sometimes get a phone call or an email that I can't automatically link to an actual or potential client. A solid trail of correspondence would be very helpful.

I also keep index cards of personal information of each account."

"Personal information?"

"Sure. A customer's hobbies… maybe something about their family – number of kids; who's in college; the family vacations. Each of these small items helps me develop a more solid relationship with the individuals. And when I send them a note about an event or piece of information that would be helpful to them, I'd like to keep a record of that as well. Using the spreadsheet is a ridiculous time waster, but I have the important information when I visit them.

I also keep a spreadsheet of orders and shipments. I have to dig through the accounting reports to get good information about order status.

I don't think I should have to do the recordkeeping."

"How much time do you think you spend on this recordkeeping?"

"I'd guess 5+- hours a week."

"How long is your average sales call? Did you say earlier that if you're lucky, a sales call could be 30 minutes? When I think of travel time etc. does that mean you might get an additional 2 calls per week if you had a good CRM and internal reporting?"

"Could be an additional 2 calls/week."

"Did we say earlier that a typical 'B' potential customer has a close rate of about 5% from first contact?"

"Yes, on average."

"Given this information, an additional 2 calls per week with a 5% close rate means 5 new 'B' customers/year without additional sales spending. Interesting."

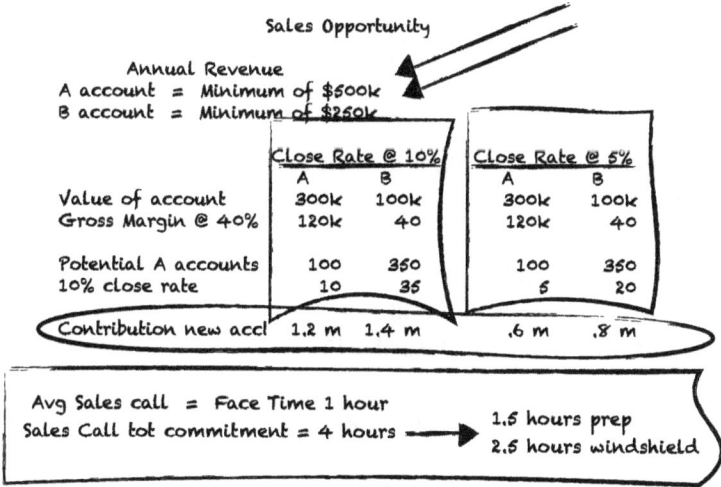

Sales Opportunity

Annual Revenue
A account = Minimum of $500k
B account = Minimum of $250k

	Close Rate @ 10%		Close Rate @ 5%	
	A	B	A	B
Value of account	300k	100k	300k	100k
Gross Margin @ 40%	120k	40	120k	40
Potential A accounts	100	350	100	350
10% close rate	10	35	5	20
Contribution new acct	1.2 m	1.4 m	.6 m	.8 m

Avg Sales call = Face Time 1 hour
Sales Call tot commitment = 4 hours ➡ 1.5 hours prep
2.5 hours windshield

"When I think of a sales call, many of them are just 'howdy' calls to keep the relationship warm. What if we had webinars to keep Precision above the radar – more visible to the A's & B's?"

"What would a webinar do for them?"

Chuck said, "I'd like to think that our engineers and sales team could come up with something 3-4 times a year to keep us above the radar.

And while I think about it, we don't do the same thing at every sales call. When I've got a prospect, I provide different information. … maybe some brochures, I might include a printout of some sections of our website… I may even show our website if there's something that would be very helpful to the potential client."

Chuck turned to Bill and Claire. "Do you vary the content of a call depending on size, and/or actual vs prospect client?"

They both agreed that the sales call will vary depending on client status and size.

"Seems like we may want to script out some core concepts depending on the sales call," Chuck continued.

Bill shuffled through some pages in his file. "Here's an example of some of the material I use. I put together a few PowerPoints that best describe Precision."

He circulated the information among attendees.

Jonathan asked, "Has Nathan reviewed this to be sure we have a consistent message to the market?"

Defensively, Bill responded, "I'm sure that this is OK. I've taken most of the information from our website."

"OK, so I'm hearing that we may have an opportunity to increase our sales calls by improved reporting and a CRM system. I think that we might want to get a core message for our standard calls – you know, the cold calls to 'A & B' accounts.

We may also want to standardize our core message to our customers."

Chuck objected. "Sounds bureaucratic to me."

"I understand your concerns about standardization. Let's look at it a different way. Each of you – Chuck, Bill and Claire – have different insight into our products, service, capabilities, and competitive advantage. It seems that each of you might be developing your own material so that you are comfortable when presenting to clients, right?"

All nodded agreement.

"What I'm suggesting is that in a very focused project, you develop the best of the best information, and be sure that marketing is involved in the process. If you set a tight deadline – for example, a 2-hour meeting – to develop the core, toss the idea to the creative folks for them to develop a useful draft.

I've seen projects like this drag on for weeks. That would be a mistake. We need to think in real time, and get a piece done quickly that may not be perfect, but will be extremely useful. Then we have the collective wisdom of all of you, and not three separate messages – and three sets of development time – to get the messaging thing done. Thoughts?"

Chuck summarized, "I'm good if we have a time limit on the development, but I sure don't want to waste weeks getting a uniform document together."

Claire and Bill agreed.

Jonathan summarized the meeting, "Chuck, this has been a great exploratory meeting. There are many opportunities available to you and the team. It seems like prioritization is the key to moving ahead.

Not only with today's resources, but once we get the new product development on board, we'll have more tools in the toolbox."

New Product Development

"I hate to leave the meeting without spending some time on new product development. I know that Randy isn't here, but can we at least spend some time on new product development?"

"Since we have Nathan here, let's do it. What are your thoughts?"

"Remember my wish list? I'd like to get some kind of flow of new products so that we have something new to talk about with our clients."

Nathan said, "I couldn't agree with you more, Chuck. How should we go about the NPD thought process, Jonathan?"

"Well, it's actually a good time to think about the new product development process. I'd like to talk about our product lines, first.

What product lines do we have today?"

"Lines? Do you mean precision castings and electronic assembly as lines?"

"That'll do. What can you tell me about the lines?"

"Precision castings are just that – cast parts using some of our proprietary processes."

"Does that include *printed* castings?"

"No such thing as a printed casting, but we have seen some developments in printed components that could substitute for our castings?"

"Like what?"

"Fixtures that are used in component alignment in turbines."

Jonathan paused for a few minutes to let people think about Nathan's response, then said, "Printed components? Should we be in that market?"

"Not sure that we can afford it, Jonathan."

"But Nathan, can we afford not to be in it? What are the economics for repetitive parts – printed versus casting?"

"Not sure. We probably should look into that."

Chuck offered, "We've seen some of the printed components come in from other than our direct competitors."

"Have these new companies been on the 'watch list' before?"

"No – our reps have seen them in the market in the last few months."

"OK – that lends credibility to getting field information from the reps. Let's continue with the NPD discussion. Should we consider three product lines? Precision cast parts, printed parts, and electronic components?"

"Since we're talking about fringe products, let me add another wrinkle. Some of our competitors have built a relationship with the customers, whereby they do more of the design work than we perform. Typically, we just accept their engineering specs, and we produce a product in response. Some competitors partner with the customers in the design phase, and actually lock in the order well before the bidding process by helping the customer design the product."

"Chuck, I agree, our engineers have great insight and design capabilities. Remember earlier I said that I met with the engineers periodically just to hear what's going on in the shop? Well, they've got what seem to be great ideas about how we can work with the customers to improve the product design."

Jonathan added, "Bill, I recall you mentioned that earlier. So, we now potentially have 3 product lines, and almost a partnership relationship with the customers. Not a bad start. Within our product lines, let's think about our individual products, and what we can do to improve our shopping basket. Any thoughts?"

Allie offered, "It's not a product, but we know the estimated life cycle of the products. Can we somehow share the information with the clients?"

Jonathan added *information* to the list.

Product Lines

Precision Castings	Metal fabrication	Other
- Aircraft	- automotive OEM	- Information
- Commercial	- office products	- International
- Defense	- appliance	- Direct
- automotive	- truck	- Distributor
- appliance	-	- Ind. Reps
- turbine		
- wind		
- hydro		
- gas		
- trucking		
-		

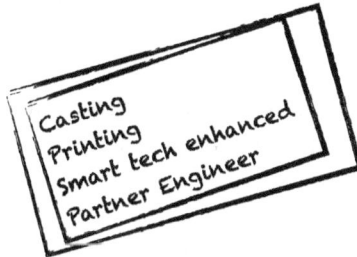

Casting
Printing
Smart tech enhanced
Partner Engineer

"That's a great list. We've covered several industries that our technology could be used in, and also several additional new products. Excellent. We won't be able to define the new products today, but this is a great start at developing new products. I think that the next step would be NPD brainstorming with Randy, Brad and Marissa.

You'll notice that I also added distribution –to International using several methods – direct, distributor, and manufacturer reps. These are several ways to penetrate the market… something to think about.

Anything else that we should talk about?"

The team was silent.

"OK. Today has been an excellent day. I'll summarize my notes from both sessions, and send them to Nathan, Chuck, and Brad.

We've accomplished a lot today. Let's say we've developed a roadmap to our future. This has not been a meeting where we defined the exact route that we will take. It's been a brainstorming session that was designed to shake the rust off… maybe create a universe of possibilities.

If there are no more questions, let's wrap this up for the day."

Jonathan adjourned the meeting, assembled his material and left the conference room. The team huddled to discuss the day's activities.

Chuck started the conversation. "Well, this has been an interesting exercise. I'm amazed at what we've tabulated as possibilities. Some seem very expensive and out of reach, while others – well, it seems that we could implement them starting tomorrow. I'm glad that Jonathan didn't think we should start anything right away, and I liked that he thought we should talk with Brad for next steps. This guy doesn't overstep his bounds."

Nathan continued. "I'm embarrassed, and grateful that he zeroed in on some of the topics. If we weren't so focused on the day-to-day, we might have been able to do this ourselves. I'll give Brad some bonus points for bringing in an outsider to shake us up a bit."

Allie and Bill were smiling. Allie was excited about the day's activities. "I am so glad that you included me in the discussion. I probably didn't add much, but it was nice to be a part of the Sales discussion."

Bill added, "Ditto. I don't have a lot of experience, but it was nice to understand how new ideas are developed. This isn't just a top-down thing – you added Allie and me into the discussion. Thank you, Chuck."

Some additional small talk, and the team dispersed.

Debrief – Brad, Nathan, and Chuck

The next morning, Brad, Nathan and Chuck met to discuss the previous days' meetings.

"I'm very glad that you were able to carve the time out of your busy schedules to meet with Jonathan. Was it worth the time?"

Nathan spoke first. "I really didn't know what to expect. I expected this old gentleman to come in and lecture us about the best way to run the business. Instead, he asked for our input. And then he dug deeper into the business. He did strike some delicate tissue. And truthfully, I was embarrassed, but he didn't grind me up. He let us sort through our opportunities.

And let' s face it, there were many things that I never considered to be within the marketing scope. Now? Well he created a monster. I'm anxious to change things, but I'm not sure where you are on this whole thing, Brad."

Chuck added, "And I also wasn't sure what to expect. Sort of the same thing … some old guy coming in telling me how I should run sales. I've been doing this for 28 years, and I wasn't optimistic about wasting a day with an uninformed outsider.

I was wrong. Just like Nathan said, he didn't pontificate, he just asked questions. Some were difficult to answer, but he didn't beat me up. He wrote a lot of information on the whiteboard. Did he share the information with you, Brad?"

"Yes, we met last night for dinner. I stuck him with the bill."

They all laughed.

"Jonathan was complimentary of you and your teams. He mentioned that you had many great ideas, and it was, 'what do we select to implement?' rather than try to develop new ideas. What do you think we should do next?"

"Brad, I'm not sure what you want to invest, but I'd like to start prioritizing some of the items that we discussed to relaunch the business."

"I'm with Chuck. We've got to prioritize the actions before we implement."

"Are you suggesting that Nathan takes his list, and begins executing… Chuck to do the same?"

Chuck jumped in, "That'll never work. This has to be a Company effort where we identify Company priorities, and not just either the sales or marketing opportunities. Agreed, Nathan?"

"Absolutely, Chuck. Couldn't have said it better. I'll use Jonathan's term – the *marketing mix* is critical. If we don't consider the impact on the Company as a whole, we're going to miss an opportunity."

"What do you suggest as the next move, Nathan?"

"I think that we need the whole executive team to meet to discuss the marketing mix. My guess is that there will be tradeoffs among us – we'll all have to dial back personal requests to get the best benefit for the Company."

"Chuck – any thoughts?"

"I agree with Nathan. But what about Randy, Marissa, Joanne, and Ben. They haven't been through the sessions with Jonathan. Is it fair to surprise them with this challenge?"

Brad thought briefly. "Maybe not fair, but what's fair. I sort of surprised you folks, and nobody shot anybody. I'll introduce the topic to each of them – they'll at least be neutral, and when I mention that you've endorsed the effort, we should be ok."

They continued the discussion, identifying areas that may be sensitive to the others. After a few minutes of additional discussion, Brad wrapped up the discussion and moved on.

Meeting – Brad, Randy, Joanne, Marissa and Ben

"I guess that you've heard the rumors. I've decided to have a workshop with a friend of mine – a consultant who's been around. We've already met with Chuck, Nathan and their team, and we're going to focus on marketing and sales."

Ben immediately mentioned, "Guess that you won't need me to attend. That's great, since I've got a lot to do in Ops."

"Now hold on, Ben. You're on the hook as well. This will be a Company meeting where we decide how to allocate resources among all the functions."

"Not sure what that has to do with manufacturing. Help me out."

"The discussions that we've had so far have enlightened all of us. When we talk about marketing, we touch on brand, new product development, communications – many other factors. When we looked at the broad array of opportunity, we saw that we might have to reallocate resources to some specific areas."

"Do you mean that you're going to cut my budget?"

"Anything is possible. We're going to work through a day's meetings to hear what we each believe to be best for the Company. That might mean we trim some budgets to invest in other functional areas, but it will be the best decision for the Company."

"Hrmph."

"And we're definitely going to be discussing new product development."

"OK. I'd like to be involved in that part of the discussion."

"And we'd like you to be involved in the entire day's discussion."

Randy perked up when he heard new product development. "Anything in particular when you mentioned new product development?"

"Yes. Our preliminary discussion shows that we need more new products… introduced flawlessly and at a quick, and predictable pace. They may be product enhancements, or entirely new products."

"OK. I get why Ops, and R&D would be involved in a marketing discussion, but why HR?"

"We were also surprised as we got into the discussion. When we explored the *brand image*, HR became part of the mix."

"I don't understand. HR doesn't produce products… doesn't sell products … doesn't interface with any customers. We're completely out of the loop."

Brad had a one-word answer. "Apple."

Joanne's puzzled look matched Marissa's.

Brad continued. "When you think of Apple, what are your thoughts?"

"Technology… classy products… great service…friendly people who are empowered."

Marissa continued, "Expensive, high margin products… produced offshore, but designed here in the US by highly trained & well-paid staff. An organization that works together to achieve success."

Joanne smiled. "That's a bit of a stretch to tie HR into that net."

Brad continued. "Is it? Apple has a culture of empowered highly trained, motivated people who know how to treat a customer. They've designed their sales & operations organization that satisfies customers… best in the business. Have you ever left an Apple discussion – in the store or on the phone… maybe even a web chat – have you ever finished a discussion angry or dissatisfied?"

"No, but to call that HR is a stretch, isn't it?"

"Who sets the HR policies? Who helps select the right people to work in the organization? Who develops the training? … develops the compensation plans … formal personnel review processes….?"

"Brad – you've convinced me. I want a raise if I have that much influence on the success of the business." She laughed out loud.

While also laughing, Randy said, "And if new products are that important to the success of the Company, I'd like a raise as well."

Brad leaned back in the chair. "Remember that bonus program that we developed a few years ago? Well, if this marketing/sales review turns out the way Jonathan thinks is possible, you'll all be receiving bonuses so large, your imagination can't take you there. I'm guessing that you're all in?"

Joanne folded her hands and placed them on the table, resolutely saying, "You've got me boss. Let's have at it."

Others nodded agreement.

Meeting – Brad and Jonathan

Jonathan settled into the back booth at the Mt. Adam's Bar & Grill, reading emails on his phone. He always arrived early just in case of potential traffic delays. Since he always had access to the web, it was not a waste of time to wait for his guest.

The waitress, Elizabeth, arrived with two menus, and asked if he wanted anything to start. "No thanks. I'll just hang out until my guest arrives. Say, do you have cherry pie today? Best in the city for sure...."

"I'll check and get back to you when your guest arrives."

For the next ten minutes, Jonathan continued to read emails.

Brad arrived, spotted Jonathan, and slipped into the booth. As if by magic, Elizabeth was there to accept a drink order. Since both had been there numerous times recently, they ordered iced teas, and their favorite sandwiches.

"And do you have cherry pie today, Elizabeth?"

"Yes sir."

"Then reserve two pieces for us. Even if my guest doesn't want his, I'll bring it home with me... can't beat the plump juicy cherries and buttery flaking pie crust."

Brad smiled, tugged at his waist line, and said, "If it's that good, who needs a diet…

Thanks for meeting with me Jonathan. As you suggested I discussed another set of meetings with the staff. I'll admit it, they were puzzled about attending a marketing & sales meeting, but when we explored the impact of brand, it was a lock. What do you suggest as next moves?"

They continued to discuss how a meeting might proceed – whiteboard, questions to the staff, and by having Marissa in attendance, they could get a reasonable fix on costs and benefits of the brainstorming.

Lunch was served, consumed, and the two anxiously awaited the cherry pie for dessert.

"What can we expect as output from the session? The folks like to know what to expect. Going into the meeting with solid expectations will improve their performance."

"Good question, Brad. When we're done, we'll have tasks outlined including rough financials and timelines for execution. I don't expect perfect plans, but there will be enough detail that the team can begin execution immediately. Do you have any other concerns?"

"I may not be smart enough to be concerned. Based on the earlier meetings, I've got 100% confidence that you can pull this off, get us focused and energized, and help me light a fire under this business.

Is the cherry pie really incredible?"

"Like you've never had before. It will literally melt in your mouth."

Elizabeth brought the gently warmed pie, and the first taste was as described... heavenly.

Given the size of the crowd, Brad rented a conference room at the club. When he arrived 30 minutes early, Jonathan was already organizing the room for best effect. Refreshments were aligned on a serving table. Small pads and pens were squared with each seat. Two easels with flip charts, an array of markers and two additional pads were ready for the meeting.

Several executives wandered in about 20 minutes before the meeting start. Jonathan met them at the door.

"Hi Chuck, Nathan. Thanks for joining me. Glad that you could make it."

Immediately thereafter, several other unknown guests arrived.

"Hi, my name is Jonathan. Thanks for joining us at this meeting."

"Hi Jonathan, my name is Marissa, and I'm the CFO. This is Joanne, VP of Human resources."

Joanne extended her hand saying, "We've been talking, and we're quite excited about being included in a marketing meeting. It's fair to say we're awaiting an education."

Jonathan smiled. "Once we get the meeting going, I think you'll recognize marketing as something you've been doing right along, but we may focus the effort during this meeting. C'mon in, find a comfortable seat and grab some refreshments."

A tall, thoughtful gentleman with round glasses entered the room. "Hello, I'm Jonathan the leader of the day's conference. I'm guessing that you're Randy, VP R&D."

"That's right. Glad to meet you Jonathan. I've heard a lot about you… done a bit of research. I'm expecting an exciting day of learning. My expectations are high just to forewarn you."

"Thanks for the heads-up. I hope that I don't disappoint."

As people poured the coffee and selected the bagels or pastries, they settled into their seats – some talking quietly… others reading last minute emails on their phones.

At 8:30, Brad brought the meeting to order.

"Folks, thanks for joining us today. As I've mentioned, I'm quite excited about the day's agenda. We've got a lot to cover, so first a quick refresher about Jonathan.

He's been in business as a consultant for about 20 years. Before that, his life was buried in a Corporate America structure that allowed him to work all over the world, in many different industries and functions. He refers to that experience as scar tissue. During the past few years he has dedicated his life to helping middle-market companies improve their business.

Today, we're going to concentrate on marketing and sales, and when we're done with the day, we'll have a list of activities that we decide are worthwhile doing. Jonathan isn't a dictator, but a facilitator.

He'll use his Socratic process to draw information from us, and help us develop manageable goals that we can actually implement. He's already warned me that he will offer my unlimited resources – that would be money – so that we focus on solutions.

When we discussed that approach, he has assured me that most often the creative ideas that are identified will generate the cash we need to do everything – in the long run." Looking directly at Jonathan, Brad added, "Right Jonathan?"

Brad paused, smiling, and then continued. "Let's get this process underway, Jonathan. It's your show."

"Thanks Brad. Wow. Now you've done it. Expectations are high, so I better deliver." Smiling, he paused briefly, looking at each attendee, nodding a personal welcome.

"First of all, I'm not a presenter, but as Brad said, a facilitator. You folks have to give me material to facilitate, so there can't be any quiet folks in the back. We all need to participate, and there is no out-of-bounds thinking. In fact, often what you think may be out-of-bounds may be exactly the right answer. Brad mentioned it and I'll reconfirm. *Brad has unlimited funds to do anything that we discuss today.*

Jonathan smiled broadly, looked at Brad, and nodded.

"Chuck, Nathan and Brad attended an earlier discussion about marketing and sales. In that session, we developed a broader understanding of marketing, and when done in the broadest sense, how marketing will impact the entire Company… every function… that's why you folks are here," while looking at Randy, Joanne, Marissa and Ben.

He launched the agenda slide that listed highlights of the last meeting.

"In our last meeting we brainstormed activities that we believed may be helpful to grow the business through marketing and sales. During that meeting, we prioritized the opportunities to those that we felt were most important. Today, we're going to focus, in priority order, on those items. That will ensure that at the end of the day, we've gotten the most out of our one-day meeting.

Does anyone have any questions?"

Marissa tapped her pen on the table top, looking for approval to speak, and then said, "This is outstanding already. Brad has never said unlimited money, so this meeting will be an absolute joy for me."

Joanne added, "Does this mean that everyone gets a raise?"

Brad responded. "We all know the compensation, bonus and phantom stock option plan. If things go the way I expect, I think that you folks will be extremely pleased with the results of this one-day investment. Jonathan. Onward."

"During the discussions we focused on sales and marketing as *business value drivers*. From the overall definition, we broke those functions into subcategories, and then again into specific actions that we could take to improve the value of Precision Technologies, Inc.

The next two slides summarize the checklist of potential action items."

Jonathan launched the slides.

"While these charts initially look a bit frightening, when we walk through them, you'll see that it's a summary of some fairly basic concepts. Our goal today is to focus on a few of the easy concepts, discuss the potential benefits of the selected items, develop an implementation plan, and then get to work. Any questions?"

Joanne asked, "Can you talk about the X's on the charts?"

Agenda	Mktng	Sales	R&D	Ops	HR	Fin/ Legal
MARKETING						
Brand	×	×	×	×	×	×
- Definition	×	×	×	×	×	×
- Personalized	×	×	×	×	×	×
- Measures	×	×	×	×	×	×
Communications						
- Inbound	×	×				
- Outbound	×	×	×			
Competition						
- Market Share	×					
- Strengths & Weaknesses	×	×	×	×	×	×
- Targets	×	×	×	×		
Product						
- Current Portfolio	×	×		×		×
- New Product Development	×	×	×	×		×
- Inside	×	×	×	×		×
- Outside	×	×	×	×		×
Promotion						
- Collateral Material	×	×	×			
- Advertising	×	×				
- Public Relations	×					
- Website	×	×	×	×	×	×

Agenda	Mktng	Sales	R&D	Ops	HR	Fin/Legal
SALES						
Sales Management						
- A-B-C		×				
- Pipeline		×				
- Definition		×				
- Management		×			×	
- CRM		×				
Sales Cycle		×				
- Existing customer						
- Potential customer						
Sales Process		×				
- Prospecting		×				
- Management		×			×	
Channels	×	×				×
- Direct	×	×				×
- Distributors	×	×				×
- Mfg Reps	×	×				×
- JV	×	×				×
- Government	×	×	×	×		×
International	×	×	×	×		×
- Canada	×	×	×	×		×
- Mexico	×	×	×	×		×
- Europe	×	×	×	×		×
- Latin America	×	×	×	×		×

"Good question, Joanne. When we looked at the topic, one question that we needed to answer is, 'Who's responsible or affected by the topic?'

In particular, when we talked about brand, we discovered that *brand is* the Company. We used Apple as a proxy, and thought about what their brand meant to the public. During the discussion, we concluded that the company brand involved people. For example, Apple could have a policy that they will be the best at everything – product design, manufacturing, logistics, customer service etc. When we thought about the brand image more deeply, we concluded that unless everyone in the company was aligned with the brand strategy, the Company would fail.

People implement and continuously reinforce the brand. That means HR hiring, training, performance measurement, financial incentive programs, compensation etc. are critical to reinforce the successful execution of *brand*."

"I agree 100%... just didn't know what it meant. Thanks, Jonathan."

"Other questions?"

"Yes. For sure we have a lot of squares in that matrix to think about... or create an action plan. How will we be able to get through this in a one-day meeting?"

"Another good question. When I work through a consulting assignment, I want to be sure to have near term results. One of our first tasks is to prioritize our efforts so that we actually accomplish something today. Once we've got some deliverables outlined, we may get together again in the next few weeks to continue the process.

The key is to work on the process so that we actually execute to a plan. I want to work at the pace that you are comfortable with, and not overpower you with wishful, blue sky ideas that can't be implemented. OK?"

Chuck said, "So let's get on with this... time's a wasting."

Jonathan discussed each major heading: Marketing – brand; communications; competition etc. His goal was to refresh or acquaint the executives with the prior meeting conclusions. After about 10 minutes, he focused on specific deliverables.

Brand

"Let's get a consensus on Precision Technologies' brand. For the next 15 minutes, the executives discussed the elements of brand, and determined that the Precision Tech's brand was one of,

"... high-quality, technology driven, premium priced manufactured products, components and services that served the industrial markets including aerospace, transportation, and utilities markets – domestic and international."

"Excellent start. When I read that definition, it seems that the core of the brand would be R&D and Operations… 'high-quality, technology-driven, manufactured products and services…' Agreed?"

All agreed.

"Let's talk about how we can fulfill the key to our brand. Andy and Ben… talk to me. What are your first thoughts when we turn the spotlight on you?"

New Product Development (NPD)

Andy was quick to respond. "Out of that entire matrix, I'll skip right to products. Existing products, and new product development, such as printed products. I think that we've got some work to do there."

Ben was quick to respond. "Sure, we need new products. We're desperate for what you described earlier as a new product pipeline, but we're more of an ad hoc or react type of Company when it comes to new products."

"OK, Ben thank you. We heard Brad say earlier that we have unlimited funds. What are your thoughts?"

Chuck chimed in. "My guys are in the market every day, listening to what's happening in the competitive pipeline. I know that they frequently talk about price as a major block to completing the sale."

"I remember that discussion from our last meeting. Didn't we conclude that old technology can't command premium pricing?"

The conversation continued among Brad, Ben, Andy and Nathan, while Jonathan wrote on the whiteboard. After about 15 minutes, Jonathan interrupted the conversation, and directed their attention to the whiteboard.

"I've been listening to your discussion and I've tried to summarize the key points. We need the reps input directly from the market. We need to understand new science; marketing will counsel us about how a new product fits our portfolio of products; finance will coach us about costs & profitability, and operations will help us determine if we can actually build the product. And of course, Brad writes the check.

We can create an incredibly complex system to get new products out the door, or we can focus. Let's look at the white board. Thoughts?"

New Product Pipeline

		When			
	What	Q1	Q2	Q3	Q4
New Product Committee		✔	✔	✔	✔
VP Sales	2-hour meeting				
VP R&D	to discuss	New Product sourcing...			
VP Marketing	newly proposed	sales reps; trade			
CEO	products; get	journals; trade			
CFO	update of in-	associations; universities;			
VP Operations	process NPD	market research			
Product rationalization	Semi-annual		✔		✔
VP Marketing	review of product				
Tech breakthrough	As appropriate,	✔	✔	✔	✔
Engineers	engineers @				

Jonathan paused to let the team think about the chart.

"What have I left out?"

"Can you explain how this is going to work? Does that mean I'm supposed to bring a new product in each quarter?"

"Not at all, Chuck. This is merely a formal communication channel for you – or anybody – to bring in new product ideas, briefly discuss the product, and get agreement about next steps. I'm suggesting that we create a review & decision committee.

We may have 3 meetings without any new product input from the reps, but that's ok. It's on the agenda."

"My engineers are sometimes off the charts with ideas for new products. Truthfully, we may have a dozen every quarter, but many just don't seem feasible."

"I understand. Given the way technology expands, it doesn't surprise me. Team, what do you think we should do?"

Marissa offered, "Seems like we should have some kind of clearing process before it hits the agenda. Maybe a preliminary review with some of the members?"

"Thoughts?"

"Could we create some kind of preliminary template discussing some of the critical details? Perhaps estimated sales and gross margins... maybe cost to develop... estimated product life?"

"I like that," Brad agreed.

Nathan suggested, "And I think that the VP responsible for the idea should do a preclearing of whatever the template requires. If an engineer is the source of the new product idea, Randy would have to sponsor the agenda item."

Ben mildly objected. "This sounds like a lot of work, Jonathan. We've got full schedules already."

"I hear you. None of us work a regular 40-hour week... probably hasn't happened in years. But let's play with this. Do we need a new product pipeline?"

"No doubt about it."

" And in our earlier discussions we said that the source of new products should include sales, marketing, engineering...right?"

All agreed.

"We agree on the source of NPD ideas. Let's take the next step. Should we just have a general discussion about every idea anyone conceives?"

Brad leaned forward. "That's a bit worrisome. If we don't have some kind of vetting process, we could burn hours every quarter on new products that don't make any sense."

"So, what's the solution?"

"Chuck said, if we're going to limit this to a 2-hour meeting, we better have some pre-clearing check before we waste the committee's time."

"OK – it looks like we all agree there should be some kind of preclearance. Do we have any kind of template for review?"

"None."

"Thanks Marissa. Is that kind of analytical thinking already done – you know, have we been thinking through the new products considering market, operations, development and launch costs, and profitability?"

"Yes – it's really just a matter of setting up a standard form with the requirements defined."

"Is that something that takes weeks to develop? Or is it more like a half-day project to get a draft together. Not a perfect, final product, but a workable solution?"

"Yes, I'd say a half-day is reasonable."

"I don't want to box you in, but is it possible to fit that half-day in during the next month?"

"Sure. I can fit a half-day in within the next month."

Ben continued the thought. "Let's say we create this form. Now before we go to the committee, somebody needs to fill the darn thing out. Who's going to do that?"

Jonathan let the question remain unanswered.

Marissa quietly said, "I guess that it might be my department to coordinate the content."

"But that really means you'll need to get market information from Nathan; ops input from Ben; feasibility from Randy, right?"

"Correct."

"Are you folks up for that?"

"Damn load of work," Ben grumbled.

"Let's review the whole concept. We're somewhat desperate for a new product pipeline... we have multiple sources of input ... the people that identify potential new products work for everybody in the room. Any objections so far?"

Silence.

"Now that we have the creative side of NPD down, should we just start spending resources on any product that pops up? Or do we want to concentrate our 2-hour meeting only on things that count?"

Nathan said, "We can't afford to waste time on ideas that won't make sense."

"How do we understand product viability?"

"Understand the market potential... potential sales and profits ... manufacturing complexity and costs... "

"That sounds like the template information."

"The choice is yours. We can skip the pre-work, or choose to concentrate only on those products that pass certain checkpoints."

Chuck smiled. "You knew we were going to end up agreeing with you...didn't you?"

"I never know the answer. I know the questions. And as a primer, Marissa, this is a format that we discussed in an earlier meeting."

All the executives leaned back in their chairs as if relieved at how they just developed a new product development process.

Jonathan continued. "So far, we've covered Brand, new product development and product rationalization. Everyone comfortable so far?"

All agreed.

"Marissa, I've got the task of developing the NPD template within the next month. Comfortable?"

"I'm OK with that."

"Nathan, I've tagged you as chairman of the committee… you ok with that?"

"Sure… let's have at it."

"Now that we have the product line covered, should we talk about promotion?"

"Let's get on with it."

Promotion

"In our earlier meetings, we identified collateral material, advertising, public relations, and website as ways to promote the business. Is that everything?"

"I don't see trade shows and seminars… maybe webinars on your list."

"Excellent points, Randy. Are you really R&D – you've got some creative chops in that technical brain? Others?"

After a moment's pause, let's talk about each one of these. Who wants to drive?"

Nathan started the conversation and Chuck enthusiastically contributed. For the next 30 minutes, ideas bubbled from all executives, as Jonathan continued to prod for more details, continuing the fast pace until ideas were exhausted. As he prodded the team, he wrote on the whiteboard.

| Promotional Mat'l | | | | |
| Who | | When | | |
Collateral material	Q1	Q2	Q3	Q4
Brochure				
– Factory capabilities	x			
– Precision casting	x			
– metal fabrication		x		
– Electronics integration			x	
New Product launch			x	
Advertising				
Casting trade journal	x	x	x	x
Metal fab trade journal	x	x	x	x
Trade show booth		x		x
– SWAG		x		x
T&E		x		x
Public relations				
Social media	x	x	x	x
Marketing communications				
– Press releases		x	x	x
– Charitable sponsorships		x		
– Community outreach		x	x	
Company outreach				
– Keyword search	x	x	x	x
White papers		x	x	x
Newsletter		x		x
Blogs	x	x	x	x
Press releases	x	x	x	x
Website				
Basic company	x			
New product launches			x	
– press releases	x	x	x	x
Videos			x	
Product demos			x	x
Reference clients				x
Webinars		x		x

At the end of the spirited discussion, he stepped back to admire his matrix.

"Well, now you've done it again. You've brainstormed for – let's see, it was about 30 minutes. And I will confess, I didn't copy all the ideas on the board, but I picked those that had the most energy and agreement. I'd be glad to add to the list, so let's spend 10 minutes on a break, and when we reconvene, I'll add anything that you like.

I've also placed an 'x' where I thought it would be appropriate. Challenge me, because I may be completely out of line. This is your plan, not mine, so don't let me box you in.

When we return from the break, we can change anything that you like. And just in general, I'm going to guess that the responsibility drops into Nathan's shop. Correct me if I'm wrong.

I've left names open, because I want Nathan to think about his staff, and inside capabilities. We'll talk about capabilities as well. All set? Let's break for 10 minutes."

The team dispersed to the refreshments and rest rooms.

Jonathan caught Brad's eye, and held up a finger to signal that he'd like to talk with him.

"Any thoughts Brad?"

"You kept your word about keeping the pace of the discussion quick. Several times I thought that we were getting bogged down in too much detail, but you let the team run. I think they needed the room to be creative.

I especially liked that you continued to push to their complete exhaustion… nothing left on the table. And the way you've summarized… picking the likely issues or priorities, and then inviting them to correct you if you've left anything major off the summary. Very clever… keeps us in line.

Overall, I like what we've accomplished in just a few hours… can't wait until we get into the sales operations.

What do you think of our team?"

"This is a very typical team. They're focused on getting their jobs done, and this gives them an opportunity to get out of the details. The initial skepticism – normal. The way they've embraced the process is very good – among the best that I've encountered. Overall, very successful so far. I hope we can continue with the same rate of accomplishment for the rest of the day."

Jonathan moved to the Danish pastries, and selected the large, sugar coated blueberry pastry and a glass of orange juice.

Competition

After the 10-minute break, the team reassembled.

Jonathan opened the session.

"We've had a very successful morning so far. Shall we continue to drive on?" Not waiting for an answer, Jonathan continued. "So far, we've covered brand, product, promotion. But before we start competition, any comments about the charts we've summarized so far."

Joanne said, "It looks like a lot of work, Jonathan. But when I think about how we will become a better Company, I'm going to reprioritize some of my routine activities. The potential results from the additional work should definitely be worth it."

Chuck added, "I like that we've formalized the team effort – including the sales force input on things like new product development. The process that we've defined seems to be a good use of our time. We're desperate for new product development. I guess I'm saying that we can't start the process soon enough."

"OK, let's get into competition. I'll start with a simple question. What is our market share?"

"I think it depends on which product line you're discussing. We've now got the precision casting, and also the electronics lines."

"And don't forget the services business," Andy added.

"Right – three product lines. Any idea what our market share is for the individual lines?"

"C'mon, Jonathan. Baited question, since we told you at the last meeting that our US and world market share were insignificant."

"You caught me, Nathan. I just wanted everyone to hear that. Now, we can say that's a bad thing – insignificant market share – or as I like to say, we have virtually unlimited potential growth. Anyone disagree?"

Joanne bobbed her head in agreement. Marissa smiled at the 'half-full' analogy.

"Now we're all in agreement that we have a small share. Are we done? Or what else should we talk about?"

Marissa offered, "Seems like we may want to talk about those companies that have the market share."

"Anything in particular?"

"Should we identify them, and maybe talk about their business?"

"OK, let's do that. Nathan, you're in charge of marketing. Let's hear a list."

Nathan called out the list that we built at the earlier meeting, and added several new companies."

"The list sounds familiar, Nathan, but it seems a bit longer than the last time. Comments?"

"After our last discussion, I decided to do a more research… talked with the sales reps about who they see in the field… some poking around in the trade rags. I've added a few."

"Anybody recognize these names? Or would you like to add any names"

Competitors

Large		Small
Alan Bradley		Chelmsfor Ltd.
HP		Jameson & Sons
United Tech	*	Northeast Supply
Thor Industries	*	Fairfield Castings
LCI	*	MidState Fabricating
Lear	*	Samson Precision Cast.
Lennox	*	Tri-city Manufacturing
Toledo	*	Jensen Supply
* GE	*	Three Brothers Mfg. Co.
* Siemens	*	Austin Precision Supply
* Bosch		
* ABB		

The team was comfortable with the list as complete.

"Now we have a great list of companies that represent – what would we say, 95% market share? What should we do next?"

"What are the asterisks for?"

"They represent companies added sine the last time we talked."

"Do we want to know who is our greatest competition?"

"Sounds like a good suggestion. Thoughts?"

Chuck tapped the table several times with his pen to get attention. "The reps tell me that Textron and Thor Industries are killing us with pricing and technology."

Nathan added, "I've heard that Jameson, Mid State and Jensen are just coasting along – no innovative products. They're just resting on their reputations and almost winding down."

"Some financial hotshot just bought Northeast Supply. Not sure what he intends to do with it."

"Why did Northeast sell out?"

"Billy, the owner, was in his early 70's and decided to just ditch the business and start traveling. I just heard when he was travelling in Peru – Machu Picchu I think – he had some kind of event. … maybe a heart attack. Almost didn't make it."

"Anything else we should talk about? Anything interesting about the grouping – large and small?"

Jonathan let the question hang silently.

"Let me ask the question a different way. Do we sell against these competitors the same way every time?"

Chuck responded. "We've got standards related to pricing the products. When we see an unusual opportunity, we'll sometimes do what it takes to get the order."

"I understand. What makes a buyer select a competitor when they need a product?"

"Size equals stability. They'll be around if there is a problem."

"Breadth of product line."

Jonathan continued to press for advantages and disadvantages in the competitive environment, while listing strengths and weaknesses on the whiteboard.

Strengths & weaknesses

	Size	Strength/Weakness		
	l	c	s	large size
	l	c	s	International
*	l	c	s	Technology
*	l	c	s	Well trained sales force
	l	c	s	Financial resources
	l	c	s	broad product line
	l	c	s	cross-selling
	sm	c	w	established relationship
*	l	c	s	ISO
	l	c	s	PhD's
*	sm	c	s	linkage to university
	l	c	w	location
	l	PT	s	location - US
*	sm	pt	s	DOD approved
	l	c	s	vendor code
	l	c	w	bureaucratic
*	l	c	s	brand

Size	Strength/Weakness		
l	c	s	personal relationships
l	c	s	responsive
l	pt	s	move on a dime
l	pt	s	flexible
l	pt	s	easy to do business
sm	pt	s	decisive
l	pt	s	subcontractors
l	pt	s	technicians
sm	pt	s	financial strength
sm	pt	s	reputation
sm	pt	s	brand
l	pt	s	not complex
sm	pt	s	brad
l	pt	s	community/local

"This looks like a great starting point. Let's review what we've done. First, we've listed the strengths and weaknesses that we observe in the marketplace. But Nathan mentioned that some of the items applied only to the large companies. I've put an "L" next to those. I've also identified by an "S" or "W" to indicate a strength or weakness.

Quite a hodgepodge of hieroglyphics – but it serves a purpose. As we talked, I had the definite impression that we could take an action to fix a weakness. For example, DOD approved. What does it take to get the Department of Defense (DOD) approval Chuck?"

"A lot of paperwork – maybe a call to our local congressman. I guess it's just a matter of making that a priority, and spending the time."

"Would that be worth the effort?"

"I'd have to look at our product lines to find out if it's justified."

"Did you mean the current *and* new products coming on line?" Jonathan couldn't help smiling when he asked the question.

"Got it, Jonathan. Never look at just what we have, but look where we're going. I surrender."

After a brief discussion about each item with an asterisk, Jonathan listed them on the whiteboard.

"I'll confess, this is my judgment, and I need your input. I think that these 5 items are things that you can concentrate on to improve your competitiveness. Any thoughts?"

```
l    c    s   Technology
l    c    s   Well trained sales force
l    c    s   ISO
sm   c    s   linkage to university
l    c    s   brand
               DOD
```

Randy focused on the first item and said, "I don't' agree that we can do much against the large companies in technology. They have comparatively unlimited resources... and simply put, we can't touch them in spending."

"I agree..."

"So why have you said that we can do something about it?"

"I'm going to play the devil's advocate. I'm going to say wherever there is a weakness, there is a strength. Perhaps not in a single line item, but did you notice that I've tagged 'linkage with the university' as a potential action area?"

"Yes... and we have a good relationship with the university. But we can't spend anywhere near what the big competitors do."

"One of our weaknesses was a lack of PhD's. Are there many PhD's at the University?"

"Sure, but they're not working for Precision."

"Have we approached them about commercializing any of their research? Or perhaps having their research assistants working with us on some unique applications that would benefit both the university and Precision?"

"We haven't done anything like that. They're a university, not a profit organization."

"Have you heard of '1819 Innovation Hub' – University of Cincinnati? Their tag line is 'Where next happens.' They've adapted to the 21st century and have started to recognize that their research can be successfully commercialized in a way to better support the institution.

Perhaps opening a dialogue with them might open some very creative products for Precision."

"Worth a try, I guess."

Chuck questioned. "What about the well-trained sales force? Are you saying that we aren't doing a good job?"

"Not at all. This is the list that we created, and it's a particular strength of the large companies. I've listed it since training is something that we can fix.

Let's talk about what we mean when we say a well-trained sales force for the big guns. Comments?'

"Sure. They have an unbelievable amount of materials to give the client at each visit. They pretty much blow us away with scientific materials discussing their capabilities. And they cross-sell some of their other divisions if they can. Sometimes they invite customers to a suite a Great American Ball Park. Not only that, they have a routine that is scary. They seem to visit our best clients about every 3 months, whether they ask for an order or not. They keep pushing that they have this great big company that can handle any of the client's needs."

"Let's focus on what you just said, Chuck. We're talking about breadth of product line, right?"

"Yes."

"And we're talking about scientific materials… and a standard routine… every 3 months… an occasional baseball game?"

"Yes."

"Let's focus. I'll challenge you for a moment. Have we talked about white papers? Maybe a whitepaper that directly impacts the potential clients? And would an excel spreadsheet take care of the routine visits? Better yet, a CRM?"

"Sure, but they are overpowering. Unlimited spending power…"

"I understand the depth of their resources. Let me ask a question. What else do the decision makers at our clients enjoy? It can't be just baseball?"

"Soccer… golf… tennis …flying…shooting clays"

"Do we have any way to satisfy their offsite interests? For example, could we rent a suite at the soccer stadium for a game without an annual commitment?

Chuck, I'm not trying to tell you we can beat them at their own game, but the reason we're here today is to create solutions, not identify reasons why we can't beat them. Look at the listing of advantages that we have. Responsive, technically oriented, access to research at the University.

In football, when the defensive line is filled with three-hundred pounders, do we run the ball up the middle challenging them directly, or do we flank them… with speed, maybe gimmicks – who knows – to beat them. I'm not picking on you, Chuck. I want us to think of solutions, and not reasons why we can't win at this challenge."

Chuck looked down as if a wounded puppy. Quietly, he responded, "I agree."

"OK, let's make a list of actions that we can take, given our current situation, and decide how we can beat the big guys."

They started to brainstorm opportunities to win the competition.

"Now let's focus on our strengths and compare ourselves to the smaller competitors. Did I hear someone say earlier that one or two of the small companies were treading water… just waiting to cash out. They don't have any fire in their belly."

"Yes. Ensign Company's owner is in his mid-70's and really just enjoys meeting with the customers and cutting deals. I might consider him a bad competitor because to get an order, he sometimes just slashes the price."

"If I were to ask how to beat him, what would we do?"

"Focus on his best customers, and do all the right things. Maybe the soccer game, skeet shooting, expensive lunches and meetings with Randy and our R&D group…

Just overwhelm the client with goodness to snatch them away."

"And if we get a few of his major clients, will he just shut down?"

"Maybe. In fact, at some point we may be able to buy him out."

"Now there's a creative solution!" Brad couldn't resist chiming into the conversation.

Beat the competitor

	Who	Q1	Q2	Q3	Q4
Technology					
- University relationship	Randy				
- White papers	Randy				
- Web site update	Marissa				
Sales force					
- CRM	Chuck				
- White papers (see above)	Randy				
- collaeral material	Nathan				
- sales training	Chuck				
- events	Chuck				
Brand					
- community support	Joanne				
- blog					

"OK, I think that we've spent enough time on this segment... and we hit on a couple of sales opportunities.

Communications

"This has been a very productive session so far. We can wrap up the marketing segment with communications. We've broken communications into 2 segments – inbound and outbound.

Thoughts about inbound?"

Chuck looked up from his pad and said, "We need to listen to the market. I have my folks trying to pry information from clients – and potential clients – about the competitors. Trying to understand if their sales force is happy or disgruntled. Maybe trying to catch some early information about new products to be released. And we should always explore what are their needs and desires?

I also want to hear about the management at the competitors. As I mentioned a few minutes ago, some of our competitors are just milking the final stages of their business before retiring or closing shop."

"Excellent, Chuck. Do we have a systematic way to collect and categorize the information? Or is it mostly ad hoc... when the reps think of it, we ask certain questions?"

"I think it's mostly ad hoc... it would probably be a good idea to have a standard requirement to ask and catalogue anything significant. I'll take a note on that."

"Other thoughts?"

Randy offered, "You've struck a nerve about cataloging information. My engineers are always reviewing scientific journals and the trade rags to understand what's happening in the market. I think that as part of that new products committee, one of my responsibilities should include that kind of inbound information."

"Excellent. Others?"

Marissa interrupted Jonathan. "IT reports to me, and I think that we should help with the inbound information, and not just be an administrative function that ensures the system is secure and works properly. We should have automatic web scans set up for competitors, current and potential clients and industry breakthroughs. Chuck, could you give us a list of companies that you'd like to monitor?"

"Glad to – thanks for offering."

Nathan added, "I think we might want to have customer satisfaction surveys at least once a year. Using something like Survey Monkey is inexpensive, and it might be a great source of information."

Marissa continued, "We're not capable of interpreting information, but I'm guessing that our competitors all have websites – many times boasting of their accomplishments. Should we assign someone the responsibility to monitor the competitor's websites?"

"For sure. Marketing will take care of that. We've now got Finance, IT, Sales and Marketing accumulating inbound information. What do we do with it?"

"What about HR? We can review websites and blogs to find out what's happening at competitors. Glass Door.com has a lot of information posted by employees about the company cultures, and work environment. And of course, LinkedIn has a wealth of information available for public consumption."

"Outstanding suggestions, Joanne. Wonderful suggestions."

"Is a summary of the information something we should cover in our monthly management meeting?"

"Not a bad idea, Chuck. But I don't want to create an administrative monster out of our monthly meetings. We want to be sure that we have a tight agenda. Maybe summary should be distributed to the management team before the meeting, and the agenda item would be to discuss only meaningful input."

"Now you're thinking, Brad. Excellent." Jonathan was very happy with the engagement discussing inbound communication. "Does this seem to be an overpowering task – just the scan and a brief summary the day before the monthly management meeting?"

Everyone agreed that the task should be done – not a major time sinkhole.

Outbound Communications

"We've made great progress. Let's shift to outbound communications. Shout out what we think should be included in outbound communications.

Nathan, Chuck, Brad and I spent some time talking about outbound communications a few weeks ago, so we've got a head start. Guys, let's shout out some of the topics that we covered then."

Jonathan selected a red marker and as quickly as he could, listed the outbound communications topics. After just 5 minutes, the pace of new ideas dwindled.

"Now that is one heck of a list. Who has questions about the list?"

Joanne observed, "I'm not sure I understand facilities? How is that outbound communications? And while I'm probing, how does community relations fit in?"

"Anyone want to handle that?"

"I'll take that Jonathan. Remember earlier when we discussed brand? Creating an all-encompassing image of who we are. I think Jonathan added those categories since our community outreach talks about our values… how we think. And I'm going to guess that the facilities represent the physical image of who we are. If we want people to believe that we're a 1st class Company, we don't want weeds growing up in our parking lot, or paint peeling from our signage."

"OK, now I understand it's a brand thing, and I know why *I* own the responsibility. And I guess I understand why I'm community relations. Thanks Nathan."

Jonathan continued. "Let's discuss who owns these actions. As usual, I've slotted in names. Any comments?"

Communications						
Inbound	Who	Monthly Meeting				
Customer FAQ's	Nathan	✓				
Surveys	Nathan	✓				
University	Randy	✓				
Potential customers	Chuck	✓				
Reps	Chuck	✓				
Blogs	Nathan	✓				
Websites	Nathan	✓				
Trade shows	Chuck	✓				
Trade Assoc meetings	Chuck	✓				
Company Websites	Nathan	✓				

Outbound Comm	Who	Monthly Meeting	Q1	Q2	Q3	Q4
Collaterl Matl	Nathan	✓				
Trade show	Nathan			✓		✓
Customer FAQ's	Nathan	✓				
Facilities	Brad		✓	✓	✓	✓
University	Randy		✓	✓	✓	✓
Community relations	Joanne		✓	✓	✓	✓
Blogs	Brad		✓	✓	✓	✓
Trade Assoc Meetings	Chuck	✓				
Company websites	Nathan	✓				
Public speaking	Brad		✓	✓	✓	✓
Community relations	Joanne		✓	✓	✓	✓
Government relations	Randy		✓	✓	✓	✓

Chuck cleared his throat and said, "I get why I'm on the Trade Association Meetings, but others attend the meetings. Randy, weren't you at the last meeting?"

Randy nodded.

"I understand your question, Chuck. I think it's more of, 'you are the point person'. That doesn't mean that others who may attend do not have a responsibility to do the 'outbound' communications thing. For example – and I may be stretching – but Randy may offer a pre-trade association meeting discussing science breakthroughs. To many smaller members of the association, this may be very helpful for them to hear, and it gives Randy a chance to strut his stuff... builds credibility for Precision.

Of course, anything like a presentation should be coordinated through you, Nathan. We may even be able to get some press in the industry journal – again reinforcing our brand – and at no cost."

Marissa observed, "I notice that many of the outbound elements have a quarterly requirement. How rigid is that?"

"Excellent question. How important is it for us to be in front of the world – customers, potential customers, the trade? I've put a target of at least once a quarter, but that frequency may not be right. It's more of a marker – you folks have to decide what's best for the Company."

Are we comfortable with the concepts? Enough discussion so that you can begin execution within the next few weeks? Yes, Randy, a question?"

"Some of these concepts are new. The university responsibility. I understand the goal, but I've never really cultivated a focused commercialization relationship with a university. Is that something that you can help me develop… some kind of scripting?"

"… glad to help, Randy. We'll work out the timing once we finish the sessions. And if anyone else needs a bit of coaching, let me know and we can sort out the task.

Marketing Mix

"Nathan and I have talked about the marketing mix offline. Nathan, how would you like to take this one.

"Absolutely Jonathan. Some of us have seen the charts about the Marketing Mix. The marketing mix typically is defined as the four P's: Product, Price, Promotion, and Place. For our definition, I'm going to use just a slight variation of the definition. We'll focus on how we spend our money to influence the customer to buy our products and services. Specifically, I'm going to focus on Promotion and Place.

We have an entire organization that influences our brand and our ability to sell and distribute product and services. We spend money on payroll and benefits, advertising and promotion, IT and website costs, inventory carrying and logistics costs.

I'm going to use all the spending – other than direct manufacturing cost – and ask, 'How can we invest our limited resources better to influence the customer's choice.

It will be a broad study that works with each of you in your functions to challenge everything that we do. I don't have any easy answers yet, but let's discuss the concept.

As a brand we want to be easy to deal with. Does that mean that we upgrade our billing system so that our customers can more easily place orders? Could be.

Does that mean our engineers could be embedded with their new product development organization to improve our relationships? Could be.

Will we change our website to better accommodate ordering? Or perhaps include videos? Or maybe reallocate marketing money to R&D so that we have a more effective technical sale capability? Could be.

After these sessions, I have a completely different concept of how marketing should interact with each of the functions. My goal is to work with the team develop the best *mix* of spending, to achieve faster, more profitable growth.

I've talked with Jonathan about the concept – a whole Company review – to improve our capabilities.

His response? *Strategic Plan*.

If we are in agreement, we'll sort out the details and define the project within the next few weeks.

Thoughts?

Brad remained silent during Nathan's discussion.

Marissa asked, "If I hear you correctly, you want to coordinate a deep dive into the functional areas to determine how we can better invest our resources. What do you expect to achieve?"

"I'm guessing, but I believe that given our small market share, we should be able to grow at double the market rate by more effective investment. Jonathan has convinced me that we have an opportunity to redeploy up to 10-15% of our expenses to more effective usage.

Chuck has taken the first step when he proposed shifting some of the workload from $100k sales reps to $40k inside sales technicians. I think that we all have that opportunity.

Jonathan has described a process that will help us improve each area incrementally – not wholesale change.

We're now selling about $100 million a year. If we change our marketing mix, is it possible to grow at 10-15% a year – more than double market rates? I'm willing to try.

Are we a go for planning the strategic review?"

All agreed that planning should proceed, with a final determination to execute the plan if it makes sense.

Jonathan stood and said, "Thanks Nathan – nice summary. Shall we move on to sales?"

Sales

"Chuck, let's spend some time on the sales agenda. How would you like me to start?"

"Start with the finish. Where are you going with this discussion?"

"To bigger and better sales opportunities. Are you on board?"

"Let's roll."

"Can you share a bit of information about the sales organization? How many reps…if you use distributors… manufacturer's representatives.

Discuss your pipeline management… call frequency and maybe the entire sales cycle. I'll encourage all of us to ask questions if he gets into areas that you don't understand. While you're talking, I'll be writing on the board. Onward, Chuck."

"Thanks for the intro, Jonathan. Brad, Nathan, Jonathan and I touched on all those topics several weeks ago, so I've had a chance to think through many of the segments more thoroughly than during our first discussion. Jonathan, if you don't mind, I'd like to do the marker work, but I'll let you use the blue marker to add notes. You OK with that?"

"Onward Chuck," as Jonathan tossed the black marker to Chuck.

For the next 45 minutes, chuck covered all the topics and occasionally answered questions posed by team members.

Sales Rep Productivity

"Now today, I'm going to prove I don't have an artistic bone in my body – bear with me team. The organization chart is simple – straightforward. Don't be alarmed, Brad. I've put a few extra squares on the board. I'd like to add 2 inside phone sales to cover the 'C' accounts for some of the routine refill orders, and also do some of the travel scheduling with the 'A & B 'accounts. They'll cost about $40k each, all in, but I'll be substituting their time for the scheduling and 'C 'class account calls that my $100k sales guys do now

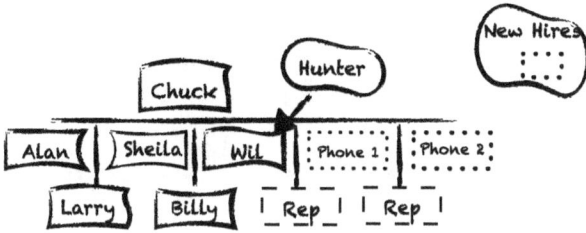

Let me take you through the analysis in rough detail. Now, this is not final, but I've talked with our sales folks, and these numbers are generally in line.

Sales Opportunity

Annual Revenue
A account = Minimum of $500k
B account = Minimum of $250k

	Close Rate @ 10%		Close Rate @ 5%	
	A	B	A	B
Potential A accounts	25	100	25	100
10% close rate	3	10	1	5
Value of account	500	250	500	250
Gross Margin @ 40%	200	100	200	100
Total Gross Margin	600	1,000	200	500
If retained for 5 years	3,000	5,000	1,000	2,500

What if we opened 3 new 'A' accounts a year for 3 years?

We've somewhat arbitrarily said that 'A' accounts are over $500k in annual volume, and focused on 'B' accounts are over $250k. We've assumed an average gross margin of 40%. Marissa, we're going to ask your help in validating or changing the number. But for now, we're going with 40%.

When we think of new accounts – I know that I'm jumping around a bit, but I want to focus on new accounts – we haven't done a great job on new accounts in the past. But for now, play along with me.

In the analysis, we've built a model with a 5% closing rate, and with a 10% closing rate. The time to close – and we're estimating once again – is about 9 months from cold call. So, let's think about this. If we're able to close on one new 'B' account in a 9-month time cycle, using a 5% close rate, we'll earn an incremental – well, as you can see, it would be major profit.

Sounds simple, right?

The question that we had to answer was how do we get that to happen? Hire a new rep at $100K? Not at first – that's a big commitment based on my soft numbers. But we do want to add the number of 'B' potential sales calls."

Brad interrupted. "How soft are your numbers? Are these 30% off…50% off?"

"Brad, they're best guess … could be off by maybe 25%.

I'll admit, Jonathan put this bug in my ear. What are those $100k reps doing all day. Again, I talked with the reps, and we found that an all-in sales call takes – maybe 5 hours. That's just 30-60 minutes – if we're lucky – in front of the potential customer, about 1.5 hours prep time, and 2.5 hours of windshield. Caution folks, these are broad averages.

So out of 5 hours of my $100k reps, only 20% is actually selling.

Digging deeper, we focused on the 1.5 hours of prep. That time is spent reviewing the last few months history of shipping, backorders, out-of-stock, open correspondence etc. We don't need the rep to do that. Thoughts?"

"Can I guess that's where the phone reps come in?"

"Yes, Joanne. And they only cost about $40k. So now, I've traded 1.5 hours of rep for more clerical support. This is a pure guess, but every week, we've estimated that the rep spends about 10 hours doing that kind of research and analysis.

I just added 2 potential sales calls to my expert reps, and I did it at a 60% reduced cost.

Follow me?"

"If you keep this up, Chuck, I'm going to draft you into the finance department." Marissa laughed as she poked at Chuck. "But it seems that you're on the right track."

Brad sat silently smiling at the analytics.

"If my estimated closing rate of 5% is anywhere near correct, and we make an additional 20 cold calls a year, we should clear more than $.5 million additional gross profit on an annual run rate … and that doesn't count what happens if we grow the accounts. Questions?"

Jonathan stood, walked to the whiteboard. "Chuck, I'm impressed. I wasn't sure we were synchronized after the last meeting, but I now see that you are a quick study. I particularly like how you've built in a bit of 'what if' with a 5% and a 10% closing rate.

I really like what you've done…. "

"Thanks Jonathan. And I've only begun."

He walked to the refreshment, opened a bottle of water, and sipped it as if it were 15-year-old scotch.

After a few minutes, he continued.

"Now that I've justified the additional inside sales, let's keep going. Here's a map of our existing coverage."

Ben laughed. "Just to be clear, you have far overstated your capability as an artist. Looks like a 5-year old with a box of crayons. Glad that you're a better sales exec than artist."

The team enjoyed Ben's observation.

"OK, big guy… wish you were on this hot seat, but your time may come.

I also want to add 2 manufacturer's reps. They're going to cover the Pac Northwest. We haven't been able to economically penetrate the area, since the customers are geographically dispersed. The manufacturer's reps will be selling other products – not us exclusively – and our margins will be lower, but a low margin on a sale is worth more than no sale and no margin.

There won't be any fixed cost… and the variable cost will be incurred only after the account receivable is collected. We've been scouting the trade to try to identify some reps, but haven't gotten too serious until we get the ok to proceed."

Marissa interrupted. "With all this fixed and variable cost discussion, I'm getting a bit nervous about losing my job to you, Chuck." All laughed.

"The manufacturer rep will concentrate on the 'A & B' potentials. Since they will already be working in the area, they'll have all the leads necessary, and we'll let the commission payment be their incentive to get 'A&B accounts.

These reps will be experienced in industrial sales, but we'll have to provide collateral material, and sales support – the phone sales folks – to keep them fully engaged.

I haven't gotten as far as I'd like, but I think we should use this same kind of model to expand to the industrial segment in Europe.

And going one step further, there are some very high-quality industrial companies in Europe that have some great complimentary products. If I get the OK, I'd like to start looking at possible distribution of some offshore products in addition to our current line."

Brad, smiling broadly, said, "You're really putting pressure on me, Chuck. But *don't* – repeat don't – let up. Make me work." Brad turned to the other execs, looked each one in the eye, and repeated, "… don't let up…"

Joanne wrote a note in her journal, "PULL ALL THE STOPS…GROW…. GROW."

Brad continued, "Are you wrapped up, or do you have more?"

Pipeline Management

"More on the way. I mentioned the pipeline. When we talked with Jonathan a few weeks ago, we talked about the pipeline. I started to think about how we approach new customers. First of all, new customers require hunters, not farmers. I'm not sure if we have the hunters on staff, but that's another discussion.

We don't have any standard approach to potential customers. I talked with the team, and we attempted to lay out a sales process."

Pipeline & Closing Cycle

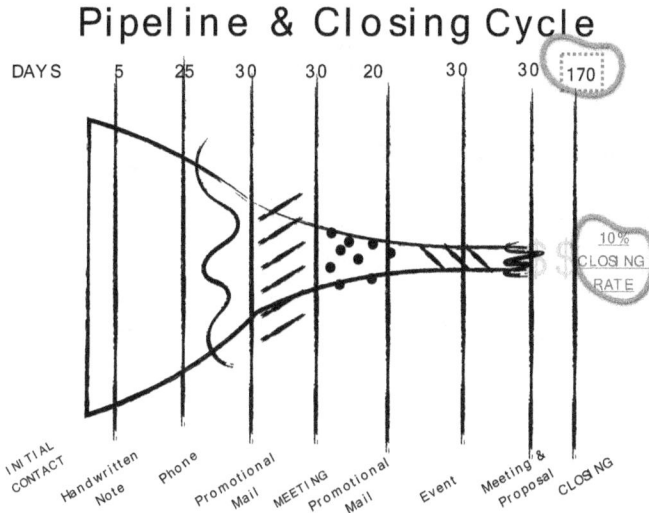

This isn't final, but we started to think through how we'd likc to sell in an ideal world. We start with a cold call. Remember those phone tech's from earlier? They'll help us identify the potential clients.

We'd start with an initial contact, and have regularly scheduled *touches* until they tell us to get lost. We expect that with a handwritten note, and a 30-day follow-up with some kind of information, we'd keep them a warm potential.

This is also where we'd like Nathan's support to scan the web for anything that might be helpful to build the relationship. If, for example, the target company just closed a big deal, the rep would send them a congratulation note to keep us above the radar. It sure doesn't hurt to have compliments from us to them.

We'd also need a reasonable supply of collateral material – maybe the occasional white paper, Randy – and some T&E to keep the wheels greased. While we haven't done the numbers, with a potential of $100k gross margin, and also thinking of the life of the customer – this could be a VERY small investment to make."

Marissa raised her pen. "Could you help me understand the life of the customer concept?"

"Great question, Marissa. I swear, I'm turning into a finance person. When we think of the life of a customer, it's really a financial evaluation of the value of sales and marketing efforts compared to a long-term customer relationship.

In the past we've evaluated pricing and promotion decisions on a transactional basis. We may provide promotional pricing to get the order. We may still do that transactional evaluation, but now we'd like to add another dimension. In the future, we'd like to think of a customer as a long-term relationship. It's complex, and while it might sound like a good way to justify a discount, we'll need your input to help us evaluate transactions and pricing strategies."

Cumulative Profit

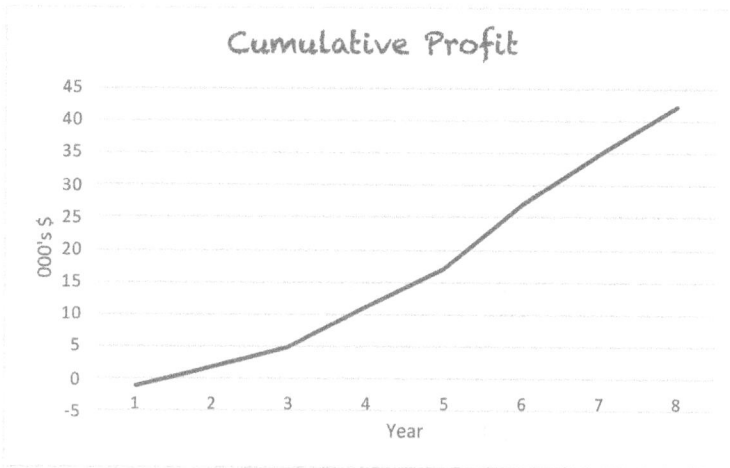

Chuck drew a chart on the board.

"This is an example. Based on our expectations for a potential 'A' customer, we might want to be more aggressive in our products or services pricing. I'm not suggesting that we sell at a loss, but we may want to trim our margins on the initial products sold into a customer to begin the partnering orientation.

For example, we may want to help them with product design – at little or no cost – to demonstrate our capabilities. Historically, we would never do that. This is a change in perspective, and not a discount program.

I'd like to work with you and Nathan to develop a process that makes sense. The benefit? If we get 10 new 'A' customers our sales just increased as a Company by up to $5 million.

Are you with me?"

"You're right, we haven't thought like this before. It makes me nervous, but if you're talking about developing a process, let's get it on the calendar."

"Do you think that we can create the template within the next month?"

"A draft template to review with Nathan and Brad? Sure."

Jonathan interrupted. "Anything else, Chuck?"

"Glad that you asked, Jonathan. I have yet to begin." Chuck walked to the whiteboard and started writing.

"I'll be working on a few other ideas – 'bout 10 I think - that we've developed in the sales operations. Now that I know we have unlimited money, we're going to really rock."

Dept of Defense
CRM
Sales training
refining call cycle
European expansion
Canada expansion
Mexico expansion
Commission for hunters
Webinars

We'll put proposals together for Marissa to look at, but I think that there are major opportunities awaiting us to grow quickly and profitably."

As Chuck was writing, Brad smiled.

"Are you the same Chuck who's been occupying the VP Sales office for the past 20+- years? *Well done*, Chuck.

Jonathan, are we there yet?"

"Brad this has been a real ride. We've ignited a firestorm within your organization. To wrap up the meeting, I'd like to summarize the commitments made so far."

He distributed pages with promises made thus far.

Some of these actions require spending, but many of them are just prioritizing existing resources to what we believe to be more valuable activities.

Let's spend a minute thinking about these. If anyone has any concerns, now's the time to raise them."

He paused as the team reviewed the summaries.

"No objections? Then let's launch this renaissance and have some fun."

ONE YEAR LATER

Although Jonathan kept losing his golf matches to Brad, they seldom discussed the business in depth during the past year. However, during the year, Jonathan worked with Randy and Nathan on specific projects to launch some of the ideas discussed in the Marketing and Sales review.

After their latest round, Brad invited Jonathan to a review. "Jonathan, a year ago we launched a marketing and sales renaissance. In celebration of this anniversary, we'd like you to join the team for a thorough update of our results.

I think that you'll be pleased with our total execution, and also surprised at the results. Remember when we first started the discussion. I was in a funk – looking to set the world on fire, but not really sure how to do so? Well, I'm on fire, Jonathan."

"I'd like to hear how the team has performed. Has it been a good year?"

"I don't want to spoil their thunder. Let's get together at the club next week. Tracey will set it up."

Celebration meeting

The conference room was prepared for the meeting. Refreshments were displayed and ready for the Precision team's arrival.

Shortly after 8 AM, the team drifted in and settled comfortably into their seats, and got their files organized. Once the papers were distributed among the seats, they moved to the refreshments.

"Joanne, what's with the multi-grain bagel?"

"Just getting health-conscious Chuck. What's up with that heavy schmeer of cream cheese?"

"I'm on an unhealthy kick. If we had some Buffalo hot sauce – you know the authentic sauce built on butter – I'd put some of that on as well." They both laughed.

At 8:30, Brad and Jonathan joined the team. Warm handshakes all around, Jonathan detected an energy he did not recall from this group. All were smiling and bubbling with discussion.

A few minutes later, Brad opened the meeting.

"Welcome to all, and especially to Jonathan. This year has been a real beauty. We've had to overcome some really major unexpected surprises. Our raw materials prices have gone through the roof with the duties on steel and aluminum… components have become very expensive due to vendor markups on sub-assemblies. But somehow, we've managed to grow – both sales and profits. It's been quite a ride.

Last year we were just short of $100 million of sales with pretax profit of $7 million, and this year – despite all the craziness – we've topped $115 million of sales with a pretax of $11 million. The team has just cashed the largest bonus checks they've ever earned, and when you look around the table, they're all smiling.

I won't tell you it's been easy. It was a year of some culture change… some very long nights to try and deliver on their commitments … but we're now in the groove and really don't have many long nights.

During the past year we've concentrated on team work centered on marketing and sales, and some great things happened.

I'm through talking. Now I'll leave it to the executives who made some magic.

Nathan – take us through the highlights."

Nathan stood and discussed the results. "Last year we launched our renaissance. As Brad mentioned, we had some rough spots, but our continuous focus was on brand as the core, and activities that supported the brand throughout the year.

After our meetings with Jonathan last year, we had a different appreciation of how the Company brand was supported by every facet of our operation. A year ago, who would believe that finance and HR could impact our brand? And yet it does, and we leveraged that knowledge.

Some of the highlights…
- Two new products introduced.
- Randy is now working closely with the university on some exotic metals and their application to our product line.
- We've opened distributors in Germany, and Italy.
- We've engaged manufacturer's reps in the Pacific Northwest.
- Our market awareness has increased geometrically through keyword search, concentrating on competitors and major clients – actual and potential.

- Our monthly management meetings now are tightly controlled, and we cover all the necessary topics in time allotted.
- We've landed 8 new 'A' accounts, thanks to a well-developed sales process concentrating on major potential accounts.
- We've increased penetration on existing accounts through a continuous flow of meaningful content using collateral materials, whitepapers, and videos to share knowledge.

These are just the highlights. Each member of the team will talk about their individual accomplishments, but we wanted to start with highlights. I'll cede the floor to Ben first.

Ben, take us on your journey."

The meeting continued for the next two hours with each executive sharing their successes and failures during the past years.

It was particularly interesting that they shared their failures – presented as learning experiences. Their transition to a performance oriented, highly competitive team was complete.

At the end of the meeting, Brad stood and looked at each executive. "My friends, we could not have achieved these results without your willingness to enthusiastically change from ingrained processes to a progressive, focused marketing and sales machine. Thank you for your help. Our renaissance only begins."

He opened his portfolio and selected 5 envelopes, one for each executive. Walking around the table, he gave an envelope to each executive, shook their hand and said, "Thank you."

Once he completed his rounds, he said, "Enclosed is a travel voucher for up to a 10-day, all expense-paid cruise of your choice. Yes, anywhere in the world. If you take the cruise within the next 12 months, the time off will not be a part of your vacation allotment – just an additional thank you for your efforts."

Smiles and 'thank you' flourished for a few minutes.

After some quiet discussion Brad adjourned the meeting.

ONLY THE BEGINNING

ABOUT THE AUTHOR

Mike Gendron (CPA-Inactive) is the founding partner of CFO Insight LLC. He has extensive experience throughout Europe, Asia and Latin America in companies ranging in size from Business Week's 'Hottest Growth Companies in America' to billion-dollar companies. Industry experience includes high-tech electronics, telecom equipment, industrial instruments and FDA regulated businesses.

During his career, he has been the CFO of global corporations – both public and private – and he has extensive experience in Fortune-500 corporations. He has participated in M&A transactions in France, Germany, China, Mexico, Canada and the US in industries such as high-tech electronics, telecom equipment, FDA regulated and industrial instruments.

He frequently speaks and writes about mergers & acquisitions, strategy, and high-growth operations, and he maintains a website (http://www.CFOInsight.net) dedicated to financial management and M&A.

In addition to flying high-performance airplanes as an instrument rated pilot, Mike enjoys backpacking, skiing and golf. Mike is Vice-Chairman of the Management & Entrepreneurship Advisory Board at Xavier University, and a member of numerous private company advisory boards.

OTHER BOOKS BY THE AUTHOR

Strategy: A Roadmap to Value
A Novel/Guide to Developing a Strategic Plan

Preserve The Value: A Novel/Guide to Successfully
Integrate an Acquisition

Cashing Out @ Full Value: A Novel/Guide for Boomers
Selling the Family Business

Doing the M&A Deal: A Quick Access Field Manual &
Guide

Creating the New E-Business Company: Innovative
Strategies for Real-World Applications

Integrating Newly Merged Organizations

A Practical Approach to International Operations

www.ingramcontent.com/pod-product-compliance
Lightning Source LLC
Chambersburg PA
CBHW020200200326
41521CB00005BA/202